Read it. Devour it. Keep it as a reference book. You'll be glad you did. *Golf's Sacred Journey* is a remarkable and encouraging story with an entirely different approach on how to excel in your golf game. Dig deep and you will realize just how much sense it makes, so much sense that you will adopt Dr. Cook's concept. I'm convinced it will improve your golf game and your life.

Zig Ziglar, leading motivational
expert and bestselling author

This book floored me. It reminded me of the many discussions David and I had during my last seven years in the NBA. The same truths I learned from him on the court are entrenched in this moving story of a young golfer who finds his purpose at the Links of Utopia. This book is full of wisdom that will enhance your game, and I believe it just may change your life.

David Robinson, NBA MVP,
two-time World Champion

This new book by Dr. Cook is one that all golfers should read. It is not only about golf, but more importantly, it is about what gives ultimate meaning in life. It is a book that will change the way you think and the way you live.

Tom Lehman, British Open Champion 1996,
U.S. Ryder Cup Captain 2006

Dave teaches what I have learned from experience, that trophies do fade and tarnish, but that relationships with God and other people are where we find true meaning and significance in our lives. I know you'll love this book as much as I did. It will give you more enjoyment, confidence, and hope on your journey around the links, and for your journey to eternity.

Scott Simpson,
U.S. Open Champion 1987

Golf's Sacred Journey is one of the best golf books I have ever read. It is a must read for anybody, especially golfers. It really touches on the mental side of the game that we all can learn from and has a wonderful spiritual message as well. You will not be able to put this book down!

Larry Mize, Master's Champion, 1987

David Cook is my friend. He has had a profound impact on my life both professionally and spiritually for many years. *Golf's Sacred Journey* has again revealed his wisdom as a teacher, coach, and encourager of life. I know that as you read this story you will not only relive your own personal successes and failures but you will take on a fresh perspective of what is truly most important to you and others you are privileged to impact. This is one trip you can't afford to miss. Enjoy the journey!

Stan Utley, PGA Tour winner
and leading short-game expert

Dr. Cook has put together a masterful story that brings psychology, physics, and theology together in this real place called Utopia. This is a must read for every parent and aspiring golfer. The words in this book will inspire you and literally change the way you approach the game and life.

Dick Coop, world-renowned mental-game
coach and author of Mind Over Golf *and* The New Golf Mind

I personally couldn't put this book down. *Golf's Sacred Journey* gives you many great insights and a different perspective to the game of golf and then finishes with truth about life.

Aaron Baddeley, PGA Tour Winner

After reading *Golf's Sacred Journey*, I felt as if a weight had been lifted off of my shoulders. I began reading in hopes of finding the secret to lower scores. Instead, I found the secret to living a meaningful life. When my days on earth are complete I'd like my headstone to read, 'Great Father ... Great Husband ... His life made a difference.' Thanks for helping me decide which way to turn.

Shaun Micheel, PGA Champion, 2003

I read this book in one sitting. It stirred my heart. What a fun and stimulating read.

Max Lucado, bestselling Christian author

This book has a simple yet wonderful message that is vital to all of us. I cannot encourage you enough to read this great book.

Jim Hardy, PGA National Teacher of the Year, 2007,
Golf Digest Top 10 Instructor

I was gripped by the tale and the principles so creatively laid out in *Golf's Sacred Journey*. David Cook is obviously not only an outstanding golf professional and mentor to many a distinguished person, David is a strategic thinker, an enthusiastic and creative storyteller, and primarily — as I have read and internalized his book — he is an exceptional guide and counselor. He encourages us to think about golf success, success in life, the primacy of that which is spiritual, and lays out tools for us to maneuver through the rocks of life.

Luis Palau, world-renowned evangelist and author,
and president of Luis Palau Association

GOLF'S SACRED JOURNEY
SEVEN DAYS AT THE LINKS OF UTOPIA

FOREWORD BY TOM LEHMAN
DAVID L. COOK
PhD

ZONDERVAN BOOKS

Golf's Sacred Journey
Copyright © 2006, 2009 by David L. Cook

Requests for information should be addressed to:
Zondervan, 3900 *Sparks Dr. SE, Grand Rapids, Michigan 49546*

Zondervan titles may be purchased in bulk for educational, business, fundraising, or sales promotional use. For information, please email SpecialMarkets@Zondervan.com.

978-0-310-36705-5 (softcover)
978-0-310-41583-1 (audio)
978-0-310-86811-8 (ebook)

Library of Congress Cataloging-in-Publication Data

Cook, David Lamar.
    Golf's sacred journey : seven days at the links of utopia / a novel by David L. Cook ; foreword by Tom Lehman.
      p. cm.
    ISBN 978-0-310-31885-9 (hardcover)
    1. Golfers—Fiction. 2. Golf stories. I. Title.
PS3603.O56885G65 2009
813'.6—dc22   2009015951

Any Internet addresses (websites, blogs, etc.) and telephone numbers in this book are offered as a resource. They are not intended in any way to be or imply an endorsement by Zondervan, nor does Zondervan vouch for the content of these sites and numbers for the life of this book.

Published in association with the literary agency of Wolgemuth & Associates, Inc.

Interior design: Christine Orejuela-Winkelman

Printed in the United States of America

HB 07.08.2022

CONTENTS

Foreword by Tom Lehman   11

Acknowledgments   15

Introduction   17

  1. A Fork in the Road   19

  2. The Links of Utopia   31

  3. Conviction   39

  4. Shadow-Casting   49

  5. Signing a Masterpiece   63

  6. Tradition vs. Truth   71

  7. Pilot's Checklist   89

  8. Hickory Sticks   103

  9. Buried Lies   123

10. A New Voice   139

11. Destiny Knocks   145

Epilogue   159

To the late Johnny Arreaga,
my childhood golf instructor,
mentor, and friend

FOREWORD BY TOM LEHMAN

A number of years ago, I heard a man say something that struck a nerve deep within my golfing soul. It was a simple truth that made complete sense.

Being a player as well as a student and observer of golf, I have seen over and over again competitors go through swing overhauls and changes because of bad rounds, a series of bad tournaments, or even because of one shot. I've never completely understood that. In my world, if you have what it takes to hit a great golf shot at some point, then it is obviously possible to do it again. I mean, if you can do it once, then you should be able to repeat it, right? It may take ten or twenty or a hundred swings to duplicate it, but that magic shot, that perfect contact followed by the perfect flight of the ball creates a feeling like no other, and once you touch it once, you want to and can touch it again. It's all about recreating the feel from those shots that you want to remember.

That's always been the way I've approached golf. A good golf swing is summed up in one word: repeatability. If you can repeat it, you can play. If what you are repeating is good enough, you can be great. It's that simple.

The words that struck me dead center in my soul were eight words spoken by Dr. David Cook, and they weren't even spoken to me but to another friend. He said: "Find what you do well and perfect it."

My whole golf experience had always been about that exact thing: not looking for a new swing, not tinkering with different swing thoughts each day, but day in and day out searching for that magic feel and the thoughts that go with it when it works.

Shots like high-drawing one-irons or drivers off the fairway or three-quarter-cut wedges that take a big hop and spin back eight feet. After I hit them once, I knew I could do it again, so my entire practice goal was to learn to repeat what worked so well. What worked well for me was a draw. I could hit the ball right to left with anyone, day in and day out, windy or calm, cold or hot. No one could draw the ball more consistently than I could. But it was sometimes a big draw, twenty yards or more. The good news is that it arrived with every swing. The club went back, the body turned through, the club followed on its assigned path, and the ball rocketed to the right and curved back toward my target. Like clockwork.

I was never inclined to try anything different, but here is the hypothetical dilemma: The coach said it curved too much, that a fade would work better at the US Open. A higher flight, increased spin, and less curve to hold those fairways and greens would work better at a major championship.

It all looked good on paper, and, after a couple weeks of work, my coach proclaimed that my swing was the best it had ever looked. The swing looked great, but the results stunk.

What's the point? Why take something that worked and exchange it for something you can't trust? How does that mesh with the wise words, "Take what you do well and perfect it"? So my plan of attack should have been to take the draw — that is who I am as a golfer — and work to draw it less and less, higher, softer, more controllable, but still a draw. That is the essence of taking what I do well and perfecting it. Those are such wise words from someone who understands competition and how important it is to trust in your method.

In this new book, David has added to the foundation of finding what you do well and perfecting it. Many people have perfected their game and have still failed miserably. Why would that be? If you can hit the shot and make it repeat, you've got the tiger by the tail, don't you? If you are strong and organized in your thinking, the answer is usually yes. But there are so many of us who get right to edge of the plane, knowing it is time to go for the gusto and jump, and we freeze at the door. We can't move, can't breathe, and the rest of the jump squad goes by, leaving us behind because of our fear.

First of all, it is understandable. Going into any unknown can be terrifying. The fear of failure incapacitates us and we are a shell of our former self. We just know that we are incapable of doing what we would like and need to do. It is a mentally induced flee response, to quit and get out of danger. And it happens weekly on the PGA Tour and anywhere else you care to look.

Here's the good news: Dr. Cook has written a book for all the people who just can't get out of their own way and are consistently their own worst enemy on the golf course. His mental checklist is: see it, feel it, trust it. His foundation is: rhythm and balance and patience.

This book about golf in Utopia is relevant to every level of golfer. I read it in less than two days. I needed to take all the wisdom it had to offer so I could apply it immediately to the 2006 AT&T Pebble

Beach National Pro-Am. See it, feel it, trust it. Patience. Create a masterpiece. I carried these words with me into the competition. The result was an attitude far less concerned with results. It was about the moment, and the result of being in the moment is momentum. It was a great place to be.

David Cook is a man of faith. He has made it perfectly clear how faith can and should interact with all areas in our life. From healing broken relationships, to seeing yourself in the right way, to being there for someone in need. Although a book about golf, the strongest part of the book may be the words about forgiveness and mercy and grace. If you are unhappy, if your life is empty and spinning out of control, then there are some ideas and answers to consider. My view of God is similar to my view of golf: He is going to take what you do well and perfect it. He's going to perform open-heart surgery on matters of deep character and turn a curse or a difficulty into a blessing.

The bottom line: Whether in golf or in life, it's time to get out of your own way and let the real you shine. If you read this book, I can assure you that you will finish it a different person than when you started.

Find what you do well and perfect it. And most of all, do it with character. Only you know your character, the person you see when you look into the mirror. Your reputation is who people think you are. Don't confuse the two. Dr. David Cook is a man of character. I have learned from him. You will, too.

ACKNOWLEDGMENTS

To all my cowboy friends in Utopia, Texas. Your pace of life and wisdom garnered from working the land and cultivating deep friendships give me new life each time I am with you.

To the Utopia Golf Course owners and staff who have provided a simple track for unpretentious folks. Thanks for reminding us of the simple pleasures of the game. It is your course that inspired this book.

To Scott Simpson for reading and editing the original manuscript, providing important insight from a seasoned player's point of view. And to Liz Worley for her tireless copyediting of the final draft.

To Bob Rotella, my friend and mentor who took me under his wing during my graduate school training in Sport Psychology so many years ago. Thanks for taking a chance on me.

To all of the amateurs, tour players, and golf professionals who have called me coach and who have lived out the words of this book. You provided the framework for the characters of the book.

To the Utopians, a group of world-class sport psychology consultants, who first met with me in Utopia in the late 1980s. Ideas for the book began to emerge during our deep discussions late into the nights on the banks of the Sabinal River in the place called Utopia.

And to my sweet wife, Karen, and children, Lexie and Hannah, for the constant encouragement and for giving me time on the front porch of the ranch house to write.

And finally to my dad who taught me the game, and to my mother for encouraging me through all the birdies, pars, and bogeys of golf and life.

INTRODUCTION

You never really know when you might meet someone who will change your life. More importantly, you never know when your influence might change another life. This book is about influence. It is about a man who lived in a simple place but had extraordinary insight. He also had something else on his side. He had time to invest himself in the life of another who was lost on his journey.

This story is based on the thousands of athletes and performers I have counseled and the great mentors and teachers from whom I have learned. I have compressed my twenty-plus years of peak performance coaching into a story of two fictional characters: a rancher with a passion for teaching truth and a young golf professional at the end of his rope. They represent each of us in the various stages of growth. In life we must be willing to coach and be coached; either one alone will leave us empty.

The setting for the book is a real place. It takes place near our ranch in the township of Utopia, Texas. Not long ago a minimalist golf course was built on the outskirts of this little village that time has passed by. The course encircles a beautiful old cemetery. One day I noticed the beginnings of what would become the golf course and driving range. I pulled up to the cemetery parking lot and observed. As I sat under the great limbs of the cemetery oaks, amused at the idea of a golf course built in the middle of nowhere, the novel began to unfold. It was an extraordinary experience, one you will share as you read the book.

The cemetery has an important role in the book. Only in a cemetery is one's life summed up with a beginning and an end. And for the blessed ones there will be an epitaph that reveals that this life made a difference.

It is my prayer that the deep truths found throughout the pages of this book will help you as you pursue your dreams in golf and life. Enjoy. And don't be surprised if you find a revolutionary hiding in your heart.

1. A FORK IN THE ROAD

How can a game have such an effect on a man's soul?

It was a scene all too familiar. I had entered this tournament with high hopes. This was going to be my breakthrough. Finally, after years of hard work and practice, my time had arrived. I entered the last round of this mini tour event within two shots of the lead. With an errant shot here, and a poor club selection there, and a three putt on the par five that I hit in two, I came to the back nine needing to make something happen. A 36 on the front left me three back with nine to go.

I began to press as I headed into the final nine. I knew better, but the adrenaline seduced my logic. Unbeknownst to me, I had just engaged the melt-down sequence.

On the tenth I pulled my shot slightly into the trees left. I pulled it because I feared the water hazard to the right. I found my ball in a small thicket of oaks. I figured I had to make a move on this nine so I decided to take a risk. After all, half the field birdied this hole on the previous day.

I saw an opening between the trees, so I tried to hit a low hook and get home in two on this short par five. Instead, it caught a limb and kicked deeper into the trees.

I couldn't just chip out now. I would be giving two shots to the field. My playing partner stood in the fairway with an iron in his hand seeming to be irritated that I was taking so long. I made a quick decision to thread the needle one more time. If I hit the green, I would still have a chance for birdie. My swing was fine but the grass behind the ball flipped the club head slightly shut, and my shot hammered a big oak, ricocheting into an area of deep grass left of the thicket. I was still out, so I hurried to find my ball. I knew it was there. I felt a panic brewing when I couldn't quickly find the ball. The grass was well above my ankles.

My playing partner was looking back at the group pushing us from behind. He was becoming angrier by the moment, not wanting our group to be put on the clock. I motioned to him to go ahead and hit. He did, and walked off in a huff after missing the green to the left. Like I had anything to do with it. He didn't come over to help. He couldn't have cared less; it wasn't his problem. His job was to beat me.

I looked back at the tee. There were two groups waiting now. I was holding up the entire field. I could feel my heart racing, the cotton was gathering in my mouth. My time was up. I had to return to the trees and drop another ball. Hurriedly, I dropped the ball without scouting out the best scenario for my drop. It landed on bare ground and bounded a few feet, resting in front of an exposed root. From my vantage point, the ball looked as if it had rolled more than two club lengths, allowing me to drop again. But I wasn't sure.

I heard the guys behind me yelling to hurry up. I saw my partner up the fairway gesturing to a rules official. I quickly grabbed a club, a seven iron, and proceeded to punch out. I picked a large opening, and without a plan in mind, hit the shot for the narrow neck of the fairway. I caught it a little thin, sending the ball scurrying across the fairway. Surely it would stop. It caught a burned out area and continued to roll toward the water hazard. I was crumbling inside. Surely this must be a dream.

The official drove up and asked why I was taking so long. Before I could answer, he said that I was on the clock and it was ticking. We went to find my ball. There it was inside the hazard, slightly nestled in greenish-brown slime at the edge of the lake. I had about 175 yards to the green. I knew I could advance it, and I felt like I might be able to get it to the green. The question was where to stand. It was wet and marshy where I needed to take my stance. On any other day I would take my shoes off and get after it, but the clock was ticking and the official had no sympathy. I grabbed a six iron and went in after it. My shoes were sinking in the mud, but I felt that I had to hit this shot. I wasn't going to wimp out now. As I took the club back my right foot sank up to my ankle. My balance was off, but I couldn't stop the swing. I tried to compensate, but there was no chance for a recovery. The club hit two inches behind the ball, catching the slime and mud. I felt the pain shoot through my left wrist all the way up to my shoulder as the club came to an abrupt stop in the thick goo. The ball moved forward a couple inches slowly sinking in the slimy water.

My shoe came off as I tried to step out of the mud. There were now three groups on the tee behind me. I was so embarrassed I wanted to quit. The official said to drop a ball and hit while he graciously helped retrieve my shoe. My shirt was covered with slime, my six iron was caked with mud, my right foot was shoeless, and I was still 175 yards from the green. My caddie threw me another ball. I dropped it and took a swing almost before it had stopped rotating on the ground. My barefoot slipped causing the ball to go low and left. It wound up in the left bunker, with a left-tucked pin. It didn't matter at that point; I was just trying to keep my sanity.

The official gave me my shoe, which was covered in dark brown muck and felt as heavy as a brick from all the water it had absorbed. I threw it to the caddy and continued to walk up the fairway with one bare foot. My playing partner had putted out for birdie and was waiting impatiently on the next tee, letting me know from his body language that I was ruining his day.

I hurriedly reached my ball in the bunker. I had a downhill lie with the green sloping away. The pin was tucked close in on the left, and a lake stared at me across the green. I was numb except for the sensation of tears building in my eyes, clouding my vision. I gave it my best shot, barely avoiding the lake. I took three putts to get home from there. I couldn't hold it in any longer. I slammed my putter into the ground, snapping it in two. The head buried deep into the earth. I screamed an obscenity and left the putter head in the ground. I was way too proud to try to dig it out in front of the gallery.

The rules official met me on the tee box and assessed me one shot for slow play and two for the tirade he just witnessed.

A couple of old college buddies saw me and ran up and asked how I was doing. They had come out to watch because they had seen that I was near the lead after day one. I yelled at them to leave me alone, not knowing they had just arrived and had not witnessed my previous hole. I was out of control. Any psychiatrist would have committed me at that moment. I had all the symptoms of a suicidal maniac. I had lost all sense of reality. In my mind I had entered a world as near to hell as you could describe.

I finished the round in what felt like a coma. I bogeyed every hole coming in. That was amazing, considering my state of mind. I didn't have a putter, and I only had one shoe on. I had no feeling.

My head was swirling. I was dying inside. I stared at my scorecard for a long time, wondering how I could disqualify myself to avoid having to post my score. But I couldn't. My dad had taught me early in life to never quit, never ever quit. There it was for everyone to see, a 15 on the hole, 12 of my shots plus three strokes tacked on by the rules official. This on the shortest par five on the course. My final score on the back was 54, to go with my 36 on the front. A 90, the worst score in the history of this tournament. That score represented me. It was my identity. I was a failure, a choke, and soon to be the butt-end of a bunch of jokes.

I jumped in my car and left the scene of the accident. I had to leave, had to drive. I was looking for an escape. I headed west out of San Antonio on a small farm-to-market road, not having a clue where it would lead me. I just knew it would be better than here, because no one would know me there. I began to cry — a grown man! I began to yell at myself, the game, and even God for allowing such a stupid game to be invented.

Mile after mile went by. I saw nothing, noticed nothing about the beauty of the Texas Hill Country in early spring. I was angry. I was despondent. I was absorbed in self-pity. It was a pathetic state of mind.

Up ahead was a fork in the road. I had to make a choice. I was in no mood to have to make a choice. The thought of it was almost overwhelming given my state of mind. I stopped. The sign's arrow pointed right, toward the small village of Vanderpool. The other arrow pointed left, toward Utopia. I read the sign again. It did say Utopia. I was desperate for anything positive to happen. I turned left, knowing it was just the name of a town, but hoping for more. I needed help. Even if it was just a name, I projected more. I was looking for an escape. So I took the road to Utopia. At the time it felt like nothing more than a fork in the road on a drive to nowhere.

DAVID L. COOK, PhD

A few miles and several curves in the road led me to Utopia, a small Hill Country town situated in the middle of what is known as the Sabinal Valley. The valley was cut out over the centuries by the clear, spring-fed Sabinal River. It is encircled by the hills of the Texas Hill Country, providing a rugged, awe-inspiring setting for a community that time has left alone. The population says 373, but my guess is they had to throw in a few deer to get the number that high. The big live oaks indigenous to that part of Texas and a traditional, small-town main street defined the town. The basic mom-and-pop businesses of grocery, mercantile, and lumber set the stage. The Lost Maple Cafe was the centerpiece.

I turned into the dusty parking area for the cafe and turned off the engine. I noticed that mine was the only car; all the other vehicles were pickup trucks or jeeps. They were all caked with the dust of the caliche roads that crisscrossed the valley from ranch to ranch. I looked into the rearview mirror to check my face for signs of tears. The last thing I needed was for some ranch-hand cowboy to see that I had been crying.

When I caught my own eyes in the mirror, time stood still. I stared into those bloodshot eyes, wondering how a man with such promise could have sunk so low. I was looking into a lost soul, empty of life. I was in a sad state of mind. How could a game affect the soul of a man so deeply?

As I opened the door of the cafe, I was enveloped with smoke and the sound of country-and-western music coming from a corner jukebox. Circles of smoke rose from half-finished cigarettes in ashtrays on most of the tables. The smoke billowed through the serving window to the kitchen, where the exhaust fans were inadequate to ventilate an establishment committed to deep-fried food.

A waitress clearing a table in lightning speed motioned to me to come in and be seated. I didn't ask for the no-smoking section. I

24

knew enough not to be laughed out of town. The place was packed, and every cowboy seemed to be looking at me. My Birkenstock sandals, khakis, and mud-stained golf shirt told everyone I was not from Utopia. Not wanting to draw additional attention to myself by standing and waiting for a table, I moved to the counter, where four old-fashioned spinning stools sat. Plastic tape held the stool's aging yellow vinyl in place. I could stare from here into the kitchen, keeping my back to the locals and the self-perceived inquisition at bay.

The waitress motioned to the blackboard for the specials of the day and asked if I wanted coffee. Before I could answer, she began to pour me a cup, saying that I looked like I could use it. She asked if I wanted a menu or wanted the special. I ordered the special, therefore avoiding further personal interaction or decision-making. The waitress turned toward the kitchen, shouting out my order, leaving me with my own thoughts.

I stared into my coffee cup, thinking back to how it had all begun. I was a twelve-year-old kid when Mr. Lux sold his land. It consisted of three hundred acres of hay and woodlands where he had raised cattle for years. Our Texas suburb sort of grew up around it, leaving an island of ranchland for my dog and me to hunt and explore. Because of numerous moves in my early years, I was somewhat of a loner still trying to find my niche. I enjoyed long afternoons in this undeveloped land with my dog. Although I had heard of unconditional love in church, my dog was the only one who expressed it.

Mr. Lux's property was bought by developers and turned into a low-budget golf course that our family quickly joined. My dad had introduced me to the game of golf several years before when I shagged balls for him at a field near the city park. He needed me to shag because the weeds were pretty thick out where I stood. I got fairly good at it using my baseball glove to catch them. I quickly learned to catch them in the web and not the palm of the glove if I wanted to use my hand the next day. While I can't say I enjoyed the scorching Texas sun, shagging balls was great practice for little league baseball. And I got to spend time with Dad, besides. When he finished practice, he always let me hit a few, patiently teaching me the fundamentals of the swing.

Dad was tough but fair. He worked extremely hard to provide the basics for our family. I knew that I was well loved. He gave my brothers and me many opportunities to participate in sports and other activities. Joining the Huaco Golf Club turned out to be a turning point in my life. I spent every waking hour at this club hitting practice balls and playing golf with an intermittent dip in the pool to cool off. I became a fixture at the club, befriending the old guys who played every day. They used to argue about who would get me on their team. I loved playing with them because they always bought me a Frosty root beer at the end of the round. I thought I was in heaven. They even paid my buddies and me to break in their new leather golf shoes. The blisters were worth every cent, because for a few days we wore the coolest shoes at the club.

As my golf game got better and better, I became the talk of the club, the kid who couldn't miss. I became somebody. I thrived on this attention and practiced harder and longer than any of the other kids. I not only wanted to be great, but the best. The people at Huaco were proud of me.

My parents saved enough to take me around to some of the area's junior tournaments. I quickly became one of the best in the region. My winning became commonplace, even expected. On the days I didn't play well, I felt people were surprised, even a little disappointed, especially around the club. I hated to disappoint anyone, so I would practice until my hands would bleed. I hated failure. It seemed that everyone thought that I was more special when I succeeded. I didn't realize it then, but I had traded unconditional love from my dog to a life of conditional acceptance based on my golf score.

The waitress slid a plate of food in front of me, along with a fork wrapped in a paper napkin. The chicken-fried steak was as tough as a boot, but the black-eyed peas, cornbread, and mashed potatoes made up for it. I was famished, and this greasy-spoon dinner was hitting the spot.

I had entered college on a golf scholarship with much anticipation. My college golf career was filled with ups and downs as I met with a new level of competition. My emotions seemed to rise and fall with my scores. If I had a good day at the course, I would be too high to sit and study. On the other hand, if I failed at the course, my mind was consumed with the mechanics of the swing. I could often be found late at night under the street lamps in the dorm parking lot practicing my swing while smacking June bugs down an imaginary fairway. Many of my phone calls home revolved around golf scores. I could sense my parents' hearts rise and fall along with my golf score. Oh, how I hated to disappoint them. They had sacrificed so much to give me the opportunity to succeed.

"Hun, do you want another cup of coffee?" My mind was a hundred miles away. I nodded. She returned with the coffee and a big piece of chocolate meringue pie that came with the special. While it looked impressive, most of it was fluff. Kind of like a girl I used to date.

My past was littered with broken relationships with girls. Golf always came between my girlfriends and me. They couldn't understand how I could be so high and low because of a game. In retrospect most of my relationships had revolved around golf. Golf was my life.

I won just enough in college to give me the confidence to turn pro. I didn't know if I could make it at the highest level, but I did know I could make it at some level. I didn't have much money, so the old men at Huaco threw in some sponsor money, as did my parents. It wasn't much but it provided a start. There were various mini-tours to choose from to get started. My ultimate goal was to play in at least one PGA Tour event someday. I wanted to tee it up with the best in the world. Maybe I would earn a spot by four-spotting. Maybe I would receive a sponsor's exemption. Lord knows I sent enough letters to tournament sponsors.

Over the past few years I drove across much of the country playing in state opens and other mini tour events. I didn't win anything of significance, but I was improving. Putting was the one skill that I knew I needed to improve to reach my dream. I was a good putter, but to make it as a pro you had to believe you were a great putter.

Every time I was about to run out of money, I would place in a tournament, earning enough to keep me going. Every time I wanted to give up, someone would offer encouraging words and tell me to hang in there. And I would hang in there, mostly because I feared what might become of me if I couldn't play golf.

This year had been a breakthrough year. I was leading the Texas Tour in earnings, which qualified me to play in the San Antonio Open at the Alamo Golf Club, an old PGA Tour stop of days gone by. The San Antonio Open was a part of the PGA Tour's developmental tour, with the winner receiving a sponsor's exemption into the Texas Open, a PGA Tour event up the road in Austin two weeks later. I was playing well. I felt like destiny was on my side. This was to be the week that I would earn my berth into a PGA event.

I arrived at the Alamo Club full of confidence. My first big junior golf victory came here at the Texas State Junior when I was sixteen. It was also the scene of my greatest golf achievement to date. I played in the state championships here my senior year in high school, shooting a 65 on the final day to win by one. It still stands as the lowest round in state championship play. The media got hold of my record at the Alamo Club and were making it a big deal. The local paper featured a story about the central Texas kid returning to the course he "owned."

I played well enough to be in contention through the first three days. I was on a high. I just knew I would make up the two shots on the last day. The front nine was shaky because of a couple of three putts. However, I still believed that I could make up the strokes on the back. My ball striking was really on. I had already written tomorrow's sports page article myself. "The kid makes up three shots on the back nine, a repeat of his high school state championship. Where was he during the Alamo?"

And then disaster struck at the tenth. Surely that was a dream, a nightmare. No one could choke that bad. Please, God, let this be a bad dream.

"Hun, can I get you anything else? Here's your check." I was in a stupor as I got up and walked to the cashier to pay. It took a few minutes for the waitress to arrive. I noticed on the wall to my left an old-fashioned bulletin board. One with several yellowed business cards that were stapled there only God knows how many years ago. Next to the cards were tacked other notices. One was for a flea market down in Sabinal. Another from a rancher who needed a ranch-hand. Another sheet was advertising a deer lease.

As the waitress appeared, my eyes caught a final notice. It was a handwritten message on a plain piece of paper. My heart stopped as I read the words. "The Links of Utopia and driving range: Find Your Game." At the bottom were directions: "Take 187 south to the Waresville turnoff. Go right and follow this for a half-mile to the cemetery. We are located next to the cemetery."

As I paid my bill, I asked the waitress if she knew anything about this course. She laughed and said that she didn't know much about golf, but a few of her regulars affectionately referred to it as Goat Ranch Country Club.

As I got into my car, I felt an inexplicable attraction to the Links of Utopia. How could a man who despised golf so much right now be remotely interested in taking a look at this course called a goat ranch by such undiscerning golfers? I felt as pitiful as an alcoholic who just wanted to smell the whiskey, knowing good and well things wouldn't stop with the sniffing.

2. THE LINKS OF UTOPIA

I pulled away from the cafe, heading south out of town and looking for the Waresville turnoff. About a mile out I saw a sign for the Waresville cemetery. I turned onto a one-lane road. About a half mile down I crossed a cattle guard and followed the lane as it curved then ended at the cemetery and the Links of Utopia golf course and driving range. I pulled up under the limbs of one of the huge oak trees that hung out from the cemetery. These trees must have been hundreds of years old. They shaded most of the cemetery with their massive limbs, giving the ancient tombstones relief from the relentless Texas sun.

I walked over to what I imagined was the driving range. At first I thought it must have been a joke. There, in the middle of a patch of weeds and rocky soil, sat three mats of Astroturf, each about six feet square. To their left was a metal pole about five feet tall with a wooden covering over it. At the base of the pole were four baskets of golf balls. Those balls were the worst-looking balls I had ever seen. They must have been used for years at another range before being rejected and given to this range. They were covered with dust, had worn dimples and illegible markings. Just above the basket of balls was a faded sign taped to the pole that read, "Five dollars for large basket. Three dollars for small basket. Put money in the slot in the pole."

I walked over to one of the Astroturf mats that rested on top of a slab of cement. About twenty yards out was a four-foot-high barbed-wire cattle fence. Between the mat and the fence was caliche dirt mixed with knee-high weeds and rocks. On the other side of the fence stretched a plowed field of dark earth. The field was about 100 yards wide and 300 yards deep. There were three worn and weathered wooden signs that read 150, 200, and 250 placed in the middle of the field. Here was the Links of Utopia driving range. I smiled for the first time that day. It really was a goat ranch.

I could see in the distance a few burned-out fairways traversing back and forth, revealing the nature of the minimalist layout of the Links of Utopia course. I noticed down the dirt road about another fifty yards a small hut about the size of an old-fashioned hamburger shop. This must be the pro shop for the nine-holer. While I wanted to laugh out loud, something seemed right about the place. A few years earlier I had traveled to Scotland and was impressed by the simplicity of the game and the locals who played it. Their courses were built into the countryside, following the lay of the land and manicured for the most part by herds of sheep. Grass was splotchy, greens were rough, and the locals were happy. They all walked and played at a very brisk pace. Maybe this old goat ranch was to the locals of Utopia as the Links of Crail was to the Scotsmen. I realized, too, that the range wasn't so much different from the field where my dad taught me the game.

It was nearing dusk, and there was no one in sight. I was ready to get out of the car anyway, so I stuffed three dollars in the slot and picked up a small bucket of balls. I opened the trunk of the car and pulled out my clubs. Just as my golf clothes had stood out in a restaurant full of ranch-hands, my clubs were no fit for this place. They were the latest in technology. The shafts were frequency matched and the lie and loft perfectly set for my address position. My driver and three-wood had graphite shafts and pushed the trampoline effect to its accepted USGA limit. My pro bag was large and leather with my name written in beautiful script on the side, revealing to everyone that I must be either a pro or a prima donna. The jury was still out on that one.

I moved to the Astroturf where I set down my bag and dumped the balls. I loosened up a little and pulled on my glove. I looked out upon the ball-pocked, dirt-clod driving range and felt a thousand miles from the disaster at the Alamo Club. I'd needed this. This session was going to be therapy for my soul. I figured I just saved myself two hundred dollars in psychologist's fees.

I looked for a decent ball to hit. Finding none, I proceeded with the one closest. I took a half swing to loosen up. The ball flew out like a dying quail, barely clearing the fence. Surely that was the ball and not my swing, I thought to myself. I hit another with the same result. These balls had seen better days. I decided to hit a few more to get warm then dig through my bag to find some real balls to hit. I hit ten more shots and only one of the balls flew true. I felt sorry for the locals who probably didn't know these balls were spent. I could only imagine what they must have felt like leaving the range.

I found about six used balls in my bag. I went to the trunk of my car and found twenty-four more. When I was a kid, I would hit thirty balls then shag them. I looked out at the 150 marker, wondering how accurate it was. I pulled out my eight-iron and sent a ball flying. It landed next to the marker.

There was a security that I felt only on the range. It was something all good players knew. That evening, as I stood on the range in Utopia, my soul was acutely aware of a reawakening, a rebirth that begins following every storm. I had felt it before but never given it much thought. I struck another ball, and it flew true to its mark. My swing felt effortless and un-judged. It was times like that evening that I could see a true measure of my talent. But I had yet to figure out if this revelation was a curse or a blessing. Golf had been the source of my greatest achievements, yet it had left scars that only time could heal. Right now I needed more time.

As I hit shot after shot with the skill of a true marksman, I was struck by the simplicity of the game. I chose a target, felt the swing, and allowed it to happen. In an environment void of pressure and expectations my body worked with the precision of a Swiss time-piece. I finished hitting my thirty balls and stared in disbelief at the grouping of balls nestled next to the 150-yard marker. The odds of a person creating this pattern with thirty dimpled balls off Astroturf with a metal stick are astronomical — unless the person has game. Oh God, why am I such a hack when it comes to posting a score when it means the most?

I carefully negotiated my way over the barbed-wire fence to re-trieve my balls. My feet sunk down into the plowed dirt filling my shoes as I trudged out to the marker. I picked the balls up one by one, flipping them up and bouncing them off the face of my sand wedge into the basket, a skill you had to perfect as a kid to be one of the "in" crowd. As I walked back, I noticed that a man had driven up to the range on his tractor, observing my every move. I worried I was going to be in trouble for climbing the fence to pick up balls to hit again without paying. Or worse, that he thought I was steal-ing range balls.

I climbed back over the fence and approached the tractor. The driver turned off the engine, wiped his brow, and climbed down. He looked about sixty years old, with dark, weathered skin. He was wearing blue jeans and boots, Texas staples, along with a well-worn US Open golf cap. His hat and khaki shirt were salt-stained from the sweat of an honest day's work. He stuck out his hand. It felt in mine like a cross between a catcher's mitt and a set of vice grips. I hung on for dear life. If you weren't ready when a Texas rancher shook your hand, you'd better pray for leniency. A man's shake was representative of his word. Though he was of average build, his strength was evidence of a life of working the land.

He had a kind face, with an air of graciousness that came from an unpretentious heart. He introduced himself as Johnny and asked if I were lost. If only he knew. Before I could answer, he said that my talent gave away my occupation. He could tell that I wasn't the typical hacker that frequented the place. He offered me a drink out of his large thermos attached to the tractor. Feeling as if he'd just caught me in a crime, I began to explain why I'd been climbing the fence. His laugh stopped me. He told me not to sweat it, that he did the same thing every evening. I asked if this was his place. He said, "Yes." As we sipped water out of paper cups in the shade of the cemetery oaks, the late afternoon sun began to retreat over the hills that encircled this place called Utopia.

Every so often in life an extraordinary relationship unfolds in a most unexpected place. I was in the midst of just such a time.

I can't explain the immediate connection I felt with this man. Maybe it was because the day had left me so in need of approval that I was desperate to connect with someone and Johnny seemed safe. Maybe it was his kindness. Maybe it was his lack of urgency to finish some task and run off to the next project that so entangles those from the city. Maybe it was the setting. Whatever the reason, time was suspended and our conversation was rich. I asked him if he was a player, a code word that we often use in golf to determine if a person is a serious golfer or a weekend hack. He replied that he could still hold his own and that in a former life he had chased the Tour a bit.

His story unfolded. He was a junior sensation before junior golf was in vogue. He dreamed of becoming a teaching pro because of the influence of his childhood pro. Along the way he won his share of amateur tournaments and eventually contended in several PGA events. But his love of teaching and his desire to spend time with his young family turned his heart homeward. He worked as an assistant for several years, eventually developing a following because of his innovative teaching methods. He believed that golf was a game, not a swing. His emphasis was always about playing the game in front of the ball, not the game behind the ball. He eventually became the head professional of the most exclusive country club in Houston.

During those years numerous pros and top amateurs found their way onto his range. His impact was significant and life-changing for many pros, but he loved teaching all levels of golfers, especially juniors. I could see something change in his expression as he talked of leaving the club that had become home for him and his family. Through the years he began to sense that something was missing. The nature of the game and business began to change — and not for the better, in his opinion. The courses had to be perfect, equipment became the rage, swing gurus seemed to emerge out of nowhere, tour pros would prostitute themselves with club companies jeopardizing their careers, and even the infomercial was courting the top teachers and players for a price. It was then that many of the players that he had coached began exploring the latest in swing gurus and theories. His simple philosophy of the game and life fell out of vogue. He lost touch with most of the players he had spent his life helping to develop, and this broke his heart.

One day he called a family meeting with his wife and two

daughters. He said that he needed a change, needed to move on, and wanted to know if they would support him. He shared his vision of finding a simple life in a small town, far away from the big city. He said that together they would head west on vacation and look for a small ranch in the Hill Country of Texas where they could run some cattle and goats. He had saved his money and invested wisely, so money wasn't a major concern. The family unanimously agreed to the adventure, and the search was on. He told me they had eventually worked their way to the same fork in the road that I had seen earlier in the day. Once they turned toward Utopia, they never looked back.

For years ranching provided a needed break from the single-mindedness of golf, but eventually something in his heart told Johnny he wasn't done with golf just yet. It was also about this time that the bottom fell out of the goat market. He was going to need a new use for the land that he had set aside for the goats. He began to let his imagination run free. He had plenty of land, a beautiful setting in the Hill Country, and a philosophy of golf and life that needed an outlet. Why couldn't he build a simple range and a nine-hole course and share his passion with the locals? After all, the nearest course was sixty miles to the north in Kerrville. To him the purest form of teaching was taking a novice and building a love for the game and an understanding of the skills required to enjoy it, even if the student was a cowboy or rancher by day.

He was now two years on the other side of the dream. Though the range and course lacked much to be desired at first sight, it was a start. Johnny was having the time of his life. While the locals affectionately referred to this place as Goat Ranch Country Club, they nevertheless came. They loved Johnny and developed an appreciation for the game of golf, even though the course seemed a bit out of place. It was indeed like a small village course in the north of

Scotland where par was a relatively new term and where the sheep were still the chief greenkeepers of the day. This was also the essence of Johnny's place, a place called the Links of Utopia. Maybe Johnny knew something that the rest of us have forgotten.

With the end of his story came the invitation. Johnny simply said, "Spend seven days with me in Utopia and you'll find your game."

While the invitation came as a surprise, destiny was on my side. I was facing a week off, so his timing couldn't have been better. It certainly began to feel like life's Composer was behind the scenes, working with renewed passion on an old, discarded symphony. This symphony would eventually, with significant help from Johnny and soul-searching from me, bring down the house in the great music hall of life.

I asked Johnny when we would begin. He said to meet him at the range at eight tomorrow morning. He directed me to the Utopia on the River Lodge, a small bed and breakfast down the road that he thought would have a room. Then he fired up his tractor and rode off into the twilight of an amazing day.

3. CONVICTION

I met Johnny at the Links of Utopia at eight on Monday morning, as promised. We started on the range, where he had set out an old-fashioned shag bag full of new Titleist golf balls, a far cry from yesterday's secondhand range balls. I warmed up on the ragged Astroturf, hitting high soft shots with a wedge just over the barbed-wire fence. The balls were landing in a poof of dust in the recently plowed cow pasture known as the range. I noticed Johnny observing my every move. He studied my grip, stance, posture, ball position with intensity. I was becoming a little self-conscious.

Finally he asked if I was warmed up. I said I was. He then asked me why I gripped the club in the manner in which I did. I said that I hadn't given it much thought, that it just felt good this way.

"Completely unacceptable," he replied.

Thinking he was talking about my grip, I asked him what was wrong with it.

He said, "The grip is fine. It is your answer that is unacceptable."

With this he pulled out a small pink note pad, scribbled my name on the top page with the word FIRED underneath, tore it off, and handed it to me. I sheepishly took the piece of paper while asking why I was being handed a pink slip at our first lesson.

"Son," he said with a certainty to his voice, "You just got fired. You are the CEO of a potential multimillion dollar company. If you want to be rehired by the end of this day you better learn to answer your board of directors with a competent and well-thought-out answer to such a strategic and crucial question. If you want to lead a successful organization, you better build a bullet-proof foundation for why you do what you do and how you do it. Or you should hang it up right now."

Before I could respond, he continued, "There is no model swing in this business, no pat answers. Each person must develop a blueprint for his swing and style of play. He must have such a conviction for the manner in which it is done that there are no chinks in the armor when facing the toughest foe on tour. The toughest challenge you will face is not necessarily the golf course, or even your competitor's scores. Your toughest foe will be the casual comment offered up by a fellow player or teacher about how you should be doing it. When I ask you about any part of your game, I want a solid answer, and I want to hear conviction in your voice. If you don't have a solid answer, I'll send you to the oak to write about it. I deeply believe that in writing our thoughts unseen wisdom rises to the occasion. I am not here to improve your swing; my purpose is to help you find your game. That is exactly what I intend to do."

He handed me a new black leather-bound journal full of blank pages. He pointed to the big oak in the cemetery about twenty yards away. He said, "I want you to take a seat under that tree and write about three things:

1. Why do you grip the club like you do?
2. Where do you play the ball in your stance for various shots?
3. What is your predominant shot pattern and why?"

I could tell that this was not going to be an ordinary lesson. Though I felt a little embarrassed, I took the book and pencil and headed for the tree. This oak was to become a friend to me during the week. It was huge, stretching its shade-producing arms in every direction. Just enough sun filtered through the limbs to provide a sense of its warming presence on my face. I sat on the grass and leaned back against the bark. I felt like I was back in school writing a paper, but this time I had a sense of urgency because this was about my livelihood. I knew he was right. I had no conviction. I had no foundation. My game changed from day to day, lesson to lesson. It seemed I had been looking everywhere but within.

I thought about the evolution of my grip. As a kid I had a very strong left hand, seeing three knuckles at address. I played a big sweeping hook and my ball flight was low, fighting the Texas winds that we faced every spring during golf season. Consequently, I played with a constant fear of the duck hook.

Being from Texas, I was always enamored of Ben Hogan and read everything I could about him. After studying Hogan and listening to all the conjecture about his so-called secret, I came up with my own theory about what turned his game around. I based my ideas on what I heard the legendary Tommy Bolt say at an outing several years back. I think it was the weakening of his left hand that transformed his career. I decided to try it out for myself. I was about twenty at the time. I knew if I wanted to compete at the highest levels I would have to overcome my fear of the hook getting away from me. Exaggerating Hogan's concept a little, I weakened my left hand until I could only see one knuckle. I also moved my left thumb from three o'clock on the top right of the shaft, to just past center on the top right of the shaft. This allowed me to pronate, or rotate the face open, on the way back for the first time in my life and protected me from over-releasing with the left hand at impact. The results were immediate and lasting. For the first time in my life I hit a high soft fade, a shot that was previously missing from my game. The hook vanished forever. I felt like I had been born again. With this new grip I could swing as hard as possible and the ball would not go left. My modified Hogan grip gave me a security blanket against the hook. From that day forward my scoring average dropped about five shots and my accuracy increased dramatically.

As far as I could tell, Hogan's left hand adjustment transformed his career, too. It is well documented that once he learned to fade the ball, he was unbeatable. When people said that Hogan's secret was that he out-practiced everyone, I knew better. Hitting one thousand low hooks a day with a poor grip wasn't going to get the job done for Hogan or for me. It was Hogan's creativity that allowed him to experiment until he understood what others would never find. Mr. Hogan, wherever you are, I was listening.

The second major transformation of my grip came when I heard an old eccentric tour pro contradict classical logic when discussing the placement of the club in the left hand. He taught to hold the club in the fingers of your left hand with the club perpendicular to your fingers (lined up with the crease marks made by the underside of the knuckles). I had spent all of my golfing life with the club angling across my palm, matching my lifeline crease, not my knuckle crease. When I made this change, it was easy for me to hinge the club at the top. I had never been able to hinge the club before. This new grip was like magic. It was simple to set the club at top. Perfect each time.

Now as I take my grip, my trademark is holding the club with my arm extended straight in front of my body, the club perpendicular to the ground, perfectly perpendicular to my fingers. This is the position I want the club at the top of my backswing. It becomes my mental anchor for the feel of the backswing.

After writing for a while, I came up for air. I was surprised at the true foundation that set my grip. Johnny was right: I needed to revisit this critical foundation of my game. It gave me confidence in my approach.

I quickly responded to the other two questions. Because of my grip change, my shot pattern was predominantly left to right; but there is no one who can hook a ball on demand better than me. I just revert to my old grip and let it rip like I did for twenty years. I have found the fade to be bulletproof. It is a safe shot that works in all situations. As far as ball position, I generally play everything off my left heel, unless playing a specialty shot. This promotes a high shot with a soft landing.

I returned to the range determined to earn my job back. I was a sucker for challenges, and Johnny had certainly gotten my attention with one. I shared my information with him. He seemed pleased. He said that it didn't really matter to him how I held the club, he was more concerned about my conviction, my heart.

"Every champion has convictions," Johnny said, "But perennial champions have convictions based on foundations. These foundations become his first line of defense when facing adversity."

I asked if I could have my job back. He chuckled and said that he would let me know next Sunday. He asked me to hit some six-irons. I hit about twenty in the pure silence of the Texas Hill Country, miles from the city and airports. Miles from a major highway. Miles from yesterday's problems. It was so quiet that the ringing in my ears became a distraction. My swing was as pure as the silence was quiet.

Finally Johnny broke the silence with a question, "What two

things do Lee Trevino, Jack Nicklaus, Arnold Palmer, and Gary Player have in common?"

I had grown up watching their careers, mostly on the senior tour. But I had read about their dramatic victories in the majors during their days on the regular Tour. They certainly didn't swing alike. They had very different personalities. They played different brands of clubs. Even their golf course design ideas contrasted.

Johnny gave me a hint. He asked, "Why do you know their names?"

I said, "Because they were successful."

"Exactly," he replied. "They kicked some tail and took no prisoners across several decades. That is the first thing they have in common. The second thing is conviction. While their swings were very different, they each had a deep belief in their own method. Those are the two common denominators: perennial success and conviction."

I kept hitting balls.

"How are you doing in those two categories?" he asked. His insight was uncanny. I was thinking about all the swing changes I had made in the past five years. Going from teacher to teacher, method to method. Trying this teaching aid and that. Switching clubs on a whim. While it seemed Hogan found his grip through his own creativity and self-exploration, I was the opposite. I was always looking for someone to give me the answer.

"To answer you honestly, I am not sure I have a method that I would take to the bank. I haven't been that successful, especially when it matters the most."

"You sure are striping the ball right now," he said as we watched another ball land in a puff of dust. "What's the deal?"

"I'm not thinking about it, I'm just swinging." I said, not realizing that I had just been led to the water.

3. Conviction

"I am a firm believer that most of us over-think the game. Golf is a game of hitting from point A to point B. Most everything else is interference. When we strip off the excess baggage, leaving the interference behind, our method becomes clear. What you are doing right now is as good as it gets. Listen to your body on this next shot. What is it saying?"

Johnny continued, "I promise I won't feed you a bunch of new-age mysticism. Hey, I'm just an old cowboy, but golf is much like the Texas two-step. Until you feel the music, you ain't nothin' but a step counter. So often we tell our body all the positions it needs to hit. While you are striping it, listen and learn from your body. This is your method. The swing is nothing but a dance. When the interference mounts, at least you will have an internal compass that will help you get back to this place."

Johnny quickly hopped up on his tractor, fired it up, and said there was some brush to clear. He said that in the Hill Country you could get a dry spring to flow again if you cleared the cedar in the area around the spring. He told me that in a sense I had the same task. He ended the lesson by saying, "Take the black book and after every few shots write something that comes to mind with regard to what you sensed or felt. Get rid of other people's words and find your own. Be creative, use word pictures, illustrations, anything that will help to return to this place and time."

There I stood on a piece of Astroturf in the middle of nowhere, hitting balls into a freshly plowed field. How did I get here? I could tell something was beginning to flow again in my soul, but I didn't understand, and I didn't have time to pursue it. I had balls to hit.

The first few shots were awful. How could you listen to your body and try to hit a shot? This intuitive stuff was new to me. I had always told my body what to do. Maybe my real problem was giving up control.

Finally I just let go and swung. The shot was pure. While I was poising over it, the first thing that came to mind was rhythm. I wrote the word rhythm in the book. I hit another shot. It was true to its target. The first thought in my mind was the word balance. My whole body seemed to move around a center. This center never wavered. Next was the word freedom. There were no hitches in the swing. I wrote the word freedom in the book. The next word was patience. So often in tournaments when I was nervous or tight, I wouldn't finish my backswing. Patience was the element I had been searching for. It was the key to completing my back swing. I excitedly wrote the word in my book.

What happened next was amazing. These and other new feelings began to lead the swing. Instead of trying to hit positions, restrict body parts, or connect the dots, I was following a different voice. It was a new voice with a new angle. I was discovering my swing. I was meeting a new coach for the first time. A dry spring was beginning to flow again.

I rediscovered that my method was about rhythm and balance more than positions. I know that I could not have gotten here without a swing teacher long ago helping to establish foundations. I just needed at some point to listen to what my body felt, rather than trying to play to another's words.

Several hours later Johnny came driving up. I was excited to tell him about the words that were transforming my game and how I approached it. Johnny shut down the engine of his old tractor and hopped down. He took off his salt-stained hat and dusted himself off, attempting to move back into the world of the golf pro. The first words out of his mouth were, "Let's see you dance cowboy."

After a few shots, he said, "Tell me about your method."

I replied, "My method is to stay balanced and to swing in

rhythm, be patient at the top, and have a sense of freedom throughout the swing."

He just smiled, gave me a pat on the back and said, "That is enough golf for the day, hop up on the back of the tractor, I want to show you something."

The day's lesson was complete. What a simple yet extraordinary experience.

He fired up the old friend and took off down a worn jeep trail. I held on tightly to the seat as we bounced along. Up ahead I saw a long line of trees that looked as though they were marching in formation. It was a narrow band of trees, different from all others, lined up along the horizon with no end in sight. As we approached them, I could see the source of their uniformity. These were the age-old cypress trees that lined the valley's water source, the Sabinal River. The Sabinal was a crystal-clear spring-fed river that flowed over a solid limestone bottom. I had never seen a stretch of water so pure.

We hopped down from the tractor at the water's edge. There was an old rope swing hanging out over the water, tied to one of the arms of an ancient cypress. I could see the bottom of the creek, though I found out it was twenty feet deep at the rope. The cypress trees shaded this lazy river by embracing the arms of the cypresses on the other bank. I could see what drew Johnny to this piece of land.

Besides golf, my other passion in life was fishing. I could see the black stripe down the side of several huge torpedoes that went drifting by, signaling to me this was a bass haven. There was a rustic canoe lying upside-down on the bank of the river. Johnny told me he wanted to see me here at seven the following morning for lesson number two. He told me to wear something that I could get wet, just in case.

"Our lesson tomorrow starts on land and moves to the canoe," he said with a smirk on his face.

He asked if I ever slowed down to just think. He said this was one of the places he came to each day just to let the experience of the day have a chance to sink in deeply. He said time to contemplate, time to listen to the learning, is crucial in the change process.

I spent the remainder of the afternoon sitting by the river. It was the first time in a long time that I had taken the time to slow down, to re-evaluate my life. It was a deep time for a guy who spent most of his time in the shallow waters of life.

4. SHADOW-CASTING

I showed up early on the banks of the cypress-lined Sabinal River. My anticipation and curiosity were piqued. The river was a soothing place, with the soft sounds of the river's flow accompanying the numerous and melodic sounds of the mockingbird. I looked carefully into the depths of the water, hoping to see the black stripe of a monster bass, the equivalent of a freshwater shark. I loved fishing for bass. I especially loved top-water action, where the bass explodes from the depths to engulf the surface intruder in a wild display of supremacy. The bass knows his role in these waters. He is the terminator. He rules supremely.

Something up-stream caught my attention. It was a canoe slowly drifting in my direction. It rode high in the water as the skipper used a sculling paddle in one arm while holding a long fly rod in the other. It was Johnny. Before I could call out to him, he brought his finger to his lips and motioned for me to sit down. Little did I know I had a front-row seat to a one-man play too extraordinary to be wasted on Broadway.

Johnny's eyes caught something in the water just ahead of the canoe. He maneuvered the craft to the center of the river with his sculling paddle. Then without a sound he let down an anchor to hold his position. He lifted the fly rod and tugged on the line to feed the leader through the eye loop until he had plenty of fly line needed for a cast. I had been in enough canoes before to know that they were as unstable as the Texas sky in late spring. Though you might get away with bait-casting or using a spinning outfit from a canoe, fly-fishing was another story. Though I had never fly-fished, it was a dream of mine. I had allowed golf to put so many dreams on hold. Some of my favorite Internet sites were those of fly-shops along the famous Colorado streams. I watched others with envy, knowing someday that I too would grace a Colorado stream during a caddis hatch, the dream of all fly-fishermen.

Johnny began the ten-o'clock-to-two-o'clock four-count rhythm of a seasoned fly-fisher at work. His artistry was impeccable, as nothing in his body appeared to move but the simple action of his arms. His eyes were focused on the prey, but his body was focused on the music. The pheasant-tailed hopper that he had strategically chosen seemed as natural as the grasshoppers that played happily in the surrounding fields. The canoe remained motionless, not producing a ripple, though the skipper's line flew in an elliptical arc from one side to the other.

I could now see a dark shape just below the surface next to the stump of a grandfather bald cypress. The fish looked huge. My heart was racing as I watched the drama unfold. The skipper continued shadow-casting just over the fish, as if to antagonize this ill-tempered predator. All the while, the skipper was calm, his focus riveted, his rhythm in sync. He was waiting patiently for the moment of truth, when he would finally let the hopper touch the surface. The fish, though, was being driven by emotion, incapable of escaping its entrapment. His fate was sealed.

Finally as if a primeval voice told him to, Johnny let the hopper gently float to the surface. It didn't make even a ripple; it was as though the hopper was alive. With a slight twitch of the rod tip, the hopper came to life. The fish could take it no longer. With the prey clearly in sight it exploded forward with a vengeance. In a fury of events Johnny snatched the hopper off the water as the huge bass exploded through the surface, leaping high in the air for the hopper only to return to the depths of the water, full of indignation at missing this simple breakfast. Johnny, on the other hand, was in control. He even had a slight grin on his face as he began the shadow-casting barrage once again. He had purposely yanked the grasshopper to gain the upper hand.

The spray from the line glistened in the early morning light, casting a surreal halo around the lead actor in the play. This entire scene had been scripted by the master; he knew the game. His patience as a hunter reminded me of the ways of the Native Americans who had graced this creek for so many years.

Meanwhile, the bass had returned to its position of attack with its tail waving excitedly at the anticipation of a second but more furious assault should the hopper return. I was consumed by the unfolding drama that revealed the stealth of the master hunter and the loss of rational control by the prey. The hunter's balance and rhythm, his sense of patience overwhelmed his urgency for the catch. While I wanted that bass in the boat right now, Johnny had faith in his strategy and was unwavering.

The moment of truth was here. With one last motion coming from the two o'clock position, the line rolled out across the water with the hopper settling ever so softly on the glassy surface. The ferocity of the strike startled me from some thirty yards away. The green monster would not be denied. Water exploded in all directions, the hopper was engulfed in the huge gaping mouth of the fish. The tail waved wildly in the air with a hang time of an NFL punt, followed by a nosedive into the depths to savor the victory and enjoy the delicacy of a Texas Hill Country hopper.

The bass had the shock of his life as his plunge was cut short by the tug of a line. The hook was set, and the fight was on. The bass instinctively headed for the brush as Johnny angled the tip of his rod toward the center of the river. Again, he was calm and in control, perfectly balanced, yet now standing in a highly unstable craft. But the fish was in a bad mood. The rod tip bent nearly to the water as Johnny held the rod high, playing the fish for all he was worth. Seeing that he couldn't make the brush, the angry fish changed his tactics and shot towards the water's surface, leaping a full two feet out of the water and shaking his head like a dog shakes water. Johnny kept the line taut, holding the tip high above his head. Back and forth the fish swam, with a force that literally rocked the canoe. Finally the bass, seized by exhaustion, could only lean against the force that was reeling him in. But when he saw the hand of the skipper reaching for his lip, he found a new reservoir of strength and made one last run. It was useless; he sensed the end and gave up the battle.

As he came to the surface, Johnny reached down and grasped the fish by his lower lip and lifted him with a smile as big as Texas. He pushed his cap back on his head, and with his other arm wiped the sweat from his brow. This had been an intense battle, culminating in the catch of a five-pounder, a giant of a fish for a clear Texas stream. Johnny worked the hook loose. Without another thought he lowered the bass back into the creek, gently moving him back and forth to rejuvenate the fish. When he let go, the fish moved slowly for a moment, assuming he was still attached to a line. Realizing he was free, he bolted for the nearest cover, licking his wounds but wiser from the battle.

Johnny pulled up anchor and paddled over to me. "Give me a hand with this canoe," he said with a smile as I pulled it up on the grass. "I've been after Toby for some time now. I finally took him out of his game." Toby, I learned, was the name the locals gave the mythical big fish in these parts. Until today, Toby was too smart to be caught.

Johnny asked me to take a seat next to an age-old cypress tree while he took a big swig from his water thermos. He wiped his mouth on his sleeve, adjusted his hat, and sat next to me. After some thought he looked at me and asked, "What did you observe?"

Knowing there was some kind of lesson about to come, I tried desperately to think of the right answer. I replied, "I just saw a man in a canoe outsmart a big bass."

"That all?" he asked, probing for more.

"Well, somehow you kept the boat from tipping or making waves while casting a fly-line. You seemed to have perfect control of the hopper. And you enticed the fish into a frenzy."

"Balance, rhythm, and patience," he exhorted.

The words were fresh in my mind. I thought back to the scene I had just witnessed. These words described the drama perfectly. The canoe remained in perfect balance throughout each cast. The only movement involved his arms, synchronized in such a way that just as his right arm contracted for the cast, his left moved forward, controlling the length of the line. As he released his right arm for the cast, his left moved toward his body. Nothing else in his body moved. The arms moving opposite each other in perfect harmony provided the physics needed for precise balance in the midst of motion. His casting rhythm was like a metronome, producing a hopper ballet. The hopper's shadow dance was mesmerizing. Johnny's patience was unflappable, enticing the fish into a frenzy.

Johnny then asked about the fish. "What was Toby's downfall?"

I thought back on the scene. The shadow-casting had enticed the fish into an emotional frenzy, leading the fish to drop his guard.

"Emotion," I replied. "A total emotional response made him vulnerable to the trap."

"Have you ever responded like that on the course?" questioned Johnny. "Dropped your guard, becoming vulnerable to a decision based on emotion?"

It didn't take much thought to realize that I played out this scene often on the course. My disappointing conclusion was that I played the role of the fish so often, though a much better role was available.

"You know, I'm more aggressive by nature and love hitting the spectacular shot. I feed upon the emotion of the game and find myself driven by the need to deliver a spectacular shot, proving to players and spectators alike that I belong. I just tend to be impatient and don't pick my spots well."

Then Johnny looked at me with a wry smile and said, "Let's get to work. If you are going to move to a new level in this game, we need to focus our attention on the variables that control and guide your game. It looks to me like rhythm, balance, and patience should be the focal points of our work today. Do you agree?"

It was hard to argue with his logic. So I simply nodded in agreement, ready to head to the range and go to work. He then handed me the fly rod and said that today's practice would take place in the canoe. My initial response was a combination of indifference, as if fishing was going to help my game, and fear of having to perform a new task in the presence of the master.

Johnny's voice broke my self-absorbed thoughts. "Let's start here in the grass. Take the rod in your right hand and grip it like you would a golf club, the V between your thumb and index finger pointing to your right shoulder. Take the line just in front of the reel in your left hand. Now modeling me, work on the ten o'clock to two o'clock motion."

For the remainder of the morning I was immersed in my first fly-fishing lesson. My immediate tendency was to start my forward cast before my back cast was complete, flip my wrist, and try to force the fly to the target. It was uncanny how it mirrored my tendencies in golf. With Johnny's great patience and wisdom I soon caught on to the point of the exercise.

Fly-fishing is all about rhythm, balance, and patience. It is an art. The fish becomes secondary. It takes a calm mindset focused on the feel of the motion rather than the outcome. Johnny was cleverly recalibrating my internal feel and profoundly changing my approach to golf.

The hopper came to life when my mind and body became calm. After a while I was dancing rather than counting my steps, playing music instead of notes. I was having fun. The transition from trying to letting was profound. Johnny directed the transition, constantly encouraging me to let the rod do the work, let the fly come alive, and let myself feel the dance. I am not sure what a prima ballerina feels during a performance, but it must be similar to what I was experiencing. Something was awakening within. The Hill Country setting was birthing a new life.

The sun shone through the wispy limbs of the cypress. The fly line was moving in a four-count rhythm, from ten to two, tracing an elegant arc through the shadow and light. All the while, Johnny's expression was one of a man in his element. A sense of simple enlightenment was seeping in to the hardness of my soul. Could it be that art had to be learned with a different heart? Could it be that golf, like fly-fishing, is art? And art is not about the outcome.

Johnny finally said that it was time to cast upon the water. It was time to let the hopper have a drink. We moved to the edge of the water to begin the process of casting. My first attempt to land the hopper without a splash was an absolute failure. It was as though I had tossed a stone into the river. The ripples reminded me of the wake of a speedboat.

Johnny, ever the teacher, asked what I was thinking. He never focused on the mechanics, for he believed that they were a reflection of a deeper source. I told him that everything changed once we moved to the water. I felt an overwhelming sense of trying to make my first cast perfect, hoping to prove that I was a good student.

"Go on," he coaxed.

"And I lost the four-count rhythm, I lost the sense of letting." I replied.

"What happened to your mechanics and form as a result?" he asked, leading me once again to the brink of discovery.

"I got short and quick. I failed to complete my back cast. And I flipped my wrist to compensate," I answered, words that echoed through the hallways of my golfing past.

"Let." He said, "Let."

I collected my thoughts, and returned to the form that had been alive just a few minutes ago while casting on land. I focused on rhythm, and on balance, and on patience. In so doing the hopper came to life and settled on the water following two patient shadow casts. The difference was dramatic. The outcome was significant. My sense of performing was transformed.

Johnny moved toward the canoe and said it was time for me to fish. "It is always more difficult to catch the second fish in the same hole, because the secret is out. Fish talk. Let's see what you're made of."

Just entering the canoe was an act of balance. It was like being on skates for the first time in years. Johnny launched me, knowing it was a matter of sinking or swimming. It was time to test the learning.

I found my sense of balance as I floated out to the center of the river, riding high in the water. I gently let down the anchor. Now it was time to test my skill. I was determined not to let my mind move off the process. I was determined to maintain my newfound technique.

I pulled out some line and carefully began to make a short and cautious shadow cast focusing on a four count, ten-to-two rhythm. I let my arms work in concert, helping me to stay balanced. The canoe was rocking a little as I learned the feel of the game in a new arena. I slowly felt the timing come together. Every ounce of my energy had to focus on letting. Rhythm, balance, and patience consumed my every pore.

Being an avid fisherman, I had a sense of where the fish were. I knew bass were territorial, so I chose a spot a bit downstream from where Johnny had taken Toby. There was a significant brush pile about five feet from an enormous cypress knee. If there was another large fish, I was convinced that this was his home.

I made about a half dozen shadow casts, getting a feel for the perfect distance to my target. My rhythm and balance were flawless. My patience was intact. The hopper landed on the water without a ripple. It was perfect, though perfection wasn't my focus. I twitched it a few times, giving life to my accomplice. I pulled the line and looked for a new landing spot, knowing that a fish surely saw the initial landing. I knew I had to continue to bombard the fish's emotions to get him to rise.

The hopper alighted once again with a realism of a hopper toppling into the water from the shore. Just then an explosion took me by surprise. A large mouth had shot from the depths of the river with a vengeance that shocked me. It was as though he thought he would win with a sneak attack. Instinctively, I jerked the rod with my upper body to set the hook.

What happened next I can't remember. All I knew was that I was submerged in a cold Texas river, sinking rapidly to the bottom of a ten-foot hole. I held the rod tightly in my hand as I began to thrash my way to the surface. I swam for the shore with one arm while pulling the rod behind me; after all I didn't want to lose Johnny's fly rod. Tangled fly line and hydrilla clung to my body like Spanish moss on the cypress. I dragged myself up on the grassy bank looking the part of a beached squid. All the while Johnny sat calmly, albeit fairly amused at this slapstick comedy scene.

"You dropped your guard," Johnny said, "You have to be ready. Otherwise, surprise gives way to emotion, and in this game emotion loses."

He was right. When the bass exploded from the depths, so did my heart. I had lost my balance in a frantic attempt to set the hook. The sneak attack won this round.

"Ever happened in golf?" asked Johnny. "Ever let a round get away because of surprise?"

It was easy to recall. Finding my ball in a divot in the middle of the fairway after a perfect drive. Having a competitor or spectator say something bizarre in the middle of the round. Having a club stolen or lost before a big round. Playing beyond my expectations. These were just a few of the sneak attacks in the game of golf that had cost me in the past.

"Emotional balance is as important as physical balance," Johnny continued. "In fact they are often woven together. To stay in balance in the canoe, or during your swing in golf, you have to have control of your emotions. You have to expect the unexpected at all times. Otherwise, you take a bath."

"You still got the hopper on that line?" he asked.

I looked for the end of the line only to find an empty tippet. Johnny helped me get untangled, added a very sheer five times tippet to the line for extra stealth fishing, and tied a new, but different colored hopper on the line.

In the meantime I waded out into the water and dragged the capsized canoe and paddles to shore.

Johnny helped me flip the vessel and reload my gear. Before I knew it, I was back on the river, searching for my wary opponent once more. I decided to try for the same fish again, knowing it would be a miracle to get him to attack a second time. But I love the ultimate challenge.

I quietly let down the anchor and began a shadow-casting barrage as I had seen earlier from the master. I never let the hopper touch the water, keeping the perpetual motion going for about ten casts, moving my target each time so that the shadow appeared and disappeared time and again. I did this to tantalize the bass and get emotion on my side this time. Finally I let the hopper alight upon the water, ready for an explosion. Nothing happened.

I repeated the casting once again. My focus was on rhythm, balance, and patience. It was as though I was in a trance. For a few moments I forgot where I was, who was watching, and how I had gotten there. It was just a rod, a fish, and me. The experience was mesmerizing. The water was like glass as the stillness of the Texas Hill Country settled around me and within me. The only sound was the whispering of the line as it danced back and forth like a hummingbird between flowers. A slight smile came across my face as I experienced the emersion beyond performing, an emersion into art.

I could sense that a fish was watching. Somehow I knew what he must be thinking: Is this real, or is it a lure? Instinctively I let the hopper alight for a millisecond then drew it off the water to continue the shadow-cast. It was part of the dance now, a sort of touch and go. I continued to do this about every third cast, seeking heightened interest from the fish. I could sense the bass's confusion grow and his emotion engage.

I had read before of the "think like a fish" method of angling, giving it about as much attention as *Caddyshack*'s "be the ball" psychobabble. However, the line between the fish and me was diminishing as I continued the chase. All the while the four-count ten-to-two rhythm was becoming automatic, freeing me to experiment with the touch-and-go method. In golf vernacular, I was shot-making.

Finally, the primeval voice was coaching me. I let the hopper alight with full expectancy of an attack. I was completely prepared to maintain composure and balance. Nothing happened. I twitched the hopper like a master puppeteer. He came to life, dancing upon the surface of the glassy water. The tiny ripples he sent out were like a web, alerting the spider that there is prey in the web. The relentless shadow-casting and touch-and-go method had unnerved the fish. The final landing and spider web dance set the anticipated eruption in motion. With nerves of steel I waited for the inevitable.

The explosion was sensational, my balance unwavering. The hook was set, and the fight was on. Deep into the water the bucketmouth darted, heading for the hydrilla and rocks below. Because of the delicate tippet I had to resist with caution, using feel over brute strength. I arrested his depth charge, changing his course of action. He headed recklessly to the surface, shaking a mighty spray high into the air. He jumped again, doing a tail dance and defying me to look in his eyes. He plunged deep and shot toward a submerged tree limb.

The anchor held but the canoe was rocking left and right with the power of his tug. I held the tip high, changing his direction once again. This time he bolted toward the canoe. I feverishly stripped off the line, trying to maintain tension. Out of the water he shot, straight at me. The tip was high above my head. With the stripping of the line I had created a pendulum, causing the momentum of the fish to careen into me and knocking me once again from the canoe. This time I didn't panic but kept the tension on as I began to sink in the water. My eyes were open in the crystal spring water. For a second I stared into the eyes of the intimidating fish. He seemed to think he had the advantage now that I was in his environment. I stayed calm as I sank to the rocks below. I knew I had enough air to play him before I surfaced. We were in the depths where the structure was and he took advantage of every opportunity to entangle the line and escape the capture. I stood weightlessly on the bottom of the river just like I had as a kid at the bottom of a swimming pool. I continued to work the fish until he showed signs of fatigue. I stripped more and more line, until the fish turned on his side about four feet away in a display of exhaustion. I reached out and grabbed his lower lip between my thumb and forefinger. I kicked my way to the surface, took one big gulp of air and then submerged to kick my way to the shallow water since my hands were occupied. Reaching the knee-deep water, I emerged victorious. A six-pound bass in one hand, Johnny's rod in the other, and an experience of a lifetime stored in my heart.

Johnny was roaring up on the sidelines, whooping and slapping his cap on his thigh. I held the bass up high, displaying him in a manner not unlike a champion of the links holding up the Claret Jug. As I held him up, we both saw, hanging from his jaw, two hoppers. I had indeed convinced the same bass to attack again — an amazing feat in the clear waters of the Sabinal.

5. SIGNING A MASTERPIECE

Johnny had asked me to meet him at the pro shop the morning of day three. The day started unlike any I have ever experienced. As I entered the makeshift pro shop, one of Johnny's assistants handed me an easel, several canvases, and an art kit full of oil paint and brushes. He told me to meet my instructor on the right side of number two fairway. I jumped in one of their old tricycle-style EZ Go golf carts and headed out, full of wonder.

The last time I had painted anything was probably third grade. All art stopped for guys around that time. Math, science, history, English, and sports became our focus. Art stopped. I never could figure out why, but I followed like a child, sure that the grownups knew what they were doing. I have to admit, something died inside around that time. Little did I know that today I would find out what that was.

I loved to draw and color as a kid. I just assumed that part of growing up was setting childish things like art aside. So I was intrigued by my cargo and anticipated what was before me.

There was no one on the course so I darted across the first

fairway and drove through the trees to the second hole. It was a par-four of medium length with one of the valley's largest oaks guarding the right side of the fairway. About three hundred yards from the tee the enormous oak was rooted well into the rough, but its majestic limbs spanned from the right quarter of the fairway through the right rough. The limbs had been trimmed up to about eight feet from the ground. Any drive lost to the right would require an under-and-around shot to a postage stamp sized green.

There behind the tree sat Johnny upon a stool, paint brush in hand, waiting for his pupil. He was wearing a big smile. In front of him was an easel and canvas. As I drove up, I could see that he was in the process of painting a picture of the oak. I wasn't surprised to see that it was exquisite. Was there anything this Renaissance man couldn't do?

He gestured to set up shop next to him. "Today's lesson starts with the canvas," he said, "and it ends with a signature."

I set up my easel, copying the master. I opened the art kit and squeezed out the primary colors onto the palette, all the while wondering what painting had to do with golf.

"I learned long ago that golf is to art like dance is to music," instructed Johnny. "Dance is a physical expression of the music; a golf shot is a physical expression of art."

He paused for a moment as he first mixed some paint then added several strokes of color to his painting, "To be a great player, you must be a great shot-maker. To be a great shot-maker, you must become an artist."

"All shots start with a blank canvas," he said as his eyes darted back and forth from the canvas to the oak. "We must paint the shot with our eyes first, before our body can produce it accurately. In essence, the quality of our shot mimics the quality of our painting."

"Here is another way to look at it." He paused, set his brush in a rusted can of turpentine, then looked back to me. "Your muscles work off of images sent from the eyes. Your muscles will hit the shot, but like a pilot in the fog, they can only respond to the information you send to them. The most powerful information is an image, a picture. A good picture produces feel and feel produces trust."

"Do you see the progression?" he asked. "First, you must see; second, you feel; third, you trust. Trust is the epitome of golf. It is the freedom to swing and let go. Great athletes compete best when they are free. Trust, you see, is earned. It is earned by feel, and feel is earned by seeing. Therefore, art is the catalyst to a great shot."

He reached for his brush, using the lip of the jar to wipe away the turpentine. "Can you see the importance of being an artist?" He backed away from his painting momentarily to gain a different perspective.

"You see," he said with the look of a philosopher, "golf is a game played to a memory. We look away from the hole, then swing. We play the game staring at a ball, yet we are attempting to move the ball to a memory, a picture that is imprinted in our minds. So it's obvious that our painting is paramount in the process. It is in fact the cornerstone."

"Let's assume our ball came to rest here, behind this tree," Johnny suggested. "What sort of shot would you hit?"

I moved behind the point he had chosen just as I would in a round of golf. I took in the entire scene. The oak dominated the landscape. I was about 120 yards to the pin. My ball rested 15 yards behind the tree, making it impossible to hit over and have enough distance to reach the green. I had to go under and curve the shot left to right about 20 yards. The limbs were trimmed up to about eight feet, so I would have to keep it low, not the easiest shot once you have opened the face. There were trees at the green, guarding the right side that must also be avoided.

"Well," I started, sort of philosophically, "it's obvious that I am in a battle with this tree. I think I would try a low punched five-iron played off my back foot with a slightly open blade. It should slice about twenty yards and roll up somewhere around the green," I said, fervently hoping he liked my shot.

"Let me ask you the question again," he said firmly but with a wry smile. "What shot will you hit? Not what shot do you think you will try. There is no room for think or try; they are deadly to commitment."

Once again I was caught in a poor word choice. Poor word choices had become a theme to my week here in Utopia. But I realized they were also a theme in my life.

With more assertiveness, I repeated the scenario with new words. "I will hit a low punched five-iron off my back foot with a slightly open face. I can see the ball flying eighty yards with a twenty-yard fade, hitting the surface with a ground-cut spin, which decreases the ball's velocity as it hops along the ground, diving to the right and up onto the green near the hole."

"Paint it," he said as he returned to mixing paint on his palette.

"Take a look at the entire setting to get your perspective," Johnny instructed. "That sets up the process."

"By the way," he added, "this great tree is not your enemy. Bunkers are not your enemy, nor are white stakes, red stakes, or yellow stakes. Water is not your enemy, nor is any object on the course. Players often look upon these inanimate objects with fear or disdain. They allow these objects to steal energy and focus. Your painting will reveal that they are just a part of the story, part of the perspective. Enjoy painting them. They will be guides that lead you to your target."

The tree dominated the landscape from where I sat. It demanded most of my attention because of its imposing size. I realized immediately that it took effort to see beyond it. Maybe that was why it was so difficult in golf to see the shot: The environment commanded attention.

Because I was painting a picture, I was able to let go of golf for a moment. A scene of unparalleled beauty unfolded in front of me. I wondered about the history of the tree, its age, the number of children that had climbed through its opened arms or picnicked under its canopy before a golf course was built around it. It seemed silly to think of the tree as an obstruction from this perspective.

Perspective was a key component to this week. Johnny was as wise as this tree was old. Everything flowed from perspective.

With that I picked up a pencil and began to sketch the scene. It wasn't long before I was erasing and starting over. This process happened several times.

Knowing exactly what was happening, Johnny said without looking up from his painting, "You have to let go of perfect to be an artist. Remember our lessons from the past two days? Your lead words were rhythm, balance, and patience. It is the same with art, you have to let go."

Johnny handed me his pencil, "Here, use this. It doesn't have an eraser. No turning back. Just see, feel, and trust."

I sketched the tree and the portion of the green I could see. I then sketched in the bottom of the flag, the only visible aspect of my target. The process was fun, yet I felt great self-consciousness. The critical voice within flowed with pessimism, but I persisted.

My palette became a creative mixing bowl of colors. I created various hues of greens and browns. My first stroke of color was somewhat timid. But with every subsequent stroke freedom found its way through my hand. I began to feel the scene and splashed color almost whimsically as I became immersed in art.

Something was loosed. Something that had long since been imprisoned was freed. The fun of painting overcame the dread of failing.

Once I laid each of the objects into the picture, I was finally ready to paint a pathway from point A to point B. Johnny was right: The objects in the painting told a story of the shot. I listened carefully as they would guide my eye.

I imagined the shot. My mind saw the low cut with a slight arc from the ground to about six feet. My aiming point, a small oak left and ten yards beyond the green, served to get the stroke started. I anticipated the knock-down five-iron flying about eighty yards with a distinctive curve to the right, taking one long hop followed by a couple of smaller ones. Finally it rolled with a slight ground spin to the right next to the hole.

I dabbed my brush in white paint and traced the imagined shot from the ball to the hole. The paint stroke was fluid and easy; my fingers and wrist were free. It was as though I were hitting the shot. The words balance, rhythm, patience, and freedom rang true.

I backed off the painting and took a look at my creation. I liked it, but something wasn't quite right. I stared at the painting then back to the scene, looking for the missing piece.

He knew. Johnny knew. In a quiet whisper he said, "It's the color." He had moved just behind me and was looking over my shoulder at the painting and the scene.

"The painting is wonderful, the color of the shot line is off. Try red. I heard that Arnie would only use red tees early on in his career. To him red meant passion, fire, aggression. Since the focal point of the painting is the shot line, let's see if the color red won't elicit a little emotion."

It was amazing how this seemingly small detail transformed the scene. The feel of the picture was altered. The meaning changed, the mood changed.

Before I knew it, Johnny handed me a five iron, tossed a ball to the grass, and said, "Every time you hit a shot, you are signing a painting. When we fail to engage art, we sign our name to a stick figure outcome."

"However," he said with a conviction that went beyond philosophy, "when you engage art, you sign your name to a masterpiece. The great ones all understand."

After a pause he simply said, "Sign it."

I moved in behind the ball. My senses were fully engaged, as I had been painting the scene for the better part of an hour. I saw the aiming point, trajectory, and shape of the shot. I could see the base of the flag, my final target. The shot line was encased in red.

As I moved into the shot and addressed the ball, I felt the shot. My club waggled as if something inside were testing the waters. The ball was back in my stance with the club face slightly open. My feet remained dynamic as I almost danced into final position. As my eyes returned to the ball, the memory was etched in my mind. The club moved off the ball as I trusted the shot. Freedom ensued.

The shot came off low and arching to the right. The deep grass hindered the spin slightly, but the shape was still there. The ball took a couple of hops, spinning to the right, rolling like a laser to its final resting spot just long and left of the flag. I had a ten-foot putt left for birdie.

I stood there, taking it in. Johnny didn't say a word. In a real sense I had just stepped back into my childhood. I was at play, and art was my companion. And it felt right.

For just a moment I saw an old picture taped to the refrigerator. It was a simple picture from a child of wonder that I had so proudly given to Mom, and there at the bottom was my name, for I always signed my paintings until the third grade. Since then I had abandoned the gift of art.

Once again the dry springs were awakened. The cedar was being cleared. Thus ended my lesson for the day; see, feel, and trust.

6. TRADITION VS. TRUTH

I t was on the fourth day that Johnny took me for a ride in his old pickup. With the windows down and country music in the background, we headed for Utopia. He said that he had some friends he wanted me to meet. We pulled up to an antique shop that specialized in old guns, knives, and war relics.

As we jumped out of the truck, I could hear music pouring from the shop. The door was wide open, as most doors in Utopia tend to be. The music had an earthy authenticity to it, its flavor somewhere between country-western and old-fashioned bluegrass. Clues of the individual instruments could be heard, yet the merger of sound created one single harmony — the essence of great music.

There was a slight haze hanging in the air, giving the open room a mystical feel. The distinct musty scent of the antiques was offset by the slight breeze ushered through the two open doors. A small spiral of smoke rose from a smoldering unfiltered cigarette on the counter. The large, floor-to-ceiling windows funneled great rays of sunlight into the room, creating light and shadows throughout. The streams of light served as rectangular spotlights where dust particles were dancing along with each chorus played.

In the center of the room sat four characters straight out of a John Wayne movie. They reclined in the dusty light from one of the windows. In many ways they blended in well with the sparse number of antiques and relics that were displayed haphazardly throughout.

Each man wore boots that hadn't seen a shine in years. Their cowboy hats were worn and stained from storms, sweat, rodeos, and such. As with all cowboys, the shape and style of the hats revealed something of each man's heart. A cowboy seldom discusses his hat; he lets it tell the story.

Noticing Johnny, the men stopped the music and stood to embrace their friend. They were kindred spirits, choosing to live in this place called Utopia rather than in the rat race down the highway. Each man was a pioneer in his own way, and each man was living his dream.

As I observed them, I sensed something else. Each of these dusty old characters, tough as a boot, were also artists. While not the painting type, they were the inspiration to the G. Harveys of the world, the great cowboy artist. These guys lived for music and poetry. In that sense, Johnny's golf course creation fit their fraternity.

Johnny introduced me to the guys. Their attention immediately turned my way. There is something about the look from a group of cowboys that makes a man feel vulnerable. They fit in this place, and I didn't. This was their stage. They held the upper hand.

The one called Jake struck a match on his boot and lighted his cigarette between his cupped hands. He took a puff. "Son," he said, "what brings you to town?"

A simple question for most, but one that caused my heart to race. The truth was that I showed up lost, distraught, and at the end of my rope. But if I said that, my manhood would be compromised.

Quickly I came up with an answer, an honest answer, thus meeting the requirement from a set of eyes that would take nothing less.

"Answers," I replied. "I am looking for answers and Johnny has them."

Johnny chimed in, "The boy's got some talent, just needs a little time in Utopia to help bring it to the surface."

Jake looked back to me, "You a musician?" he asked.

"No, I am a golfer, trying to make it on tour," I answered.

The four musicians looked over at Johnny with big grins on their faces. "Want us to give him the putting lesson?" Jake asked.

"Yep, you got it," Johnny replied. "You guys have some time this morning?"

With a bounce in their steps, they set down their instruments and headed for the register in the shop. Jake bellowed, "Who needs change?"

Quickly, money began to fly as twenties were being changed into ones.

"Son," Jake said to me, "putting lessons can get expensive in these parts. You're probably going to need some change. Got any twenties? It takes two to get into this game."

Having no clue what I was getting into, I nevertheless reached into my wallet and pulled out a couple of twenties. Jake handed me twenty one-dollar bills and four five-dollar bills.

A putting lesson, I thought to myself. What were they talking about? What could four cowboy musicians teach me about putting?

The cowboys exited out the back door. It emptied into a beautiful back yard surrounded by a picket fence that lost its white many years ago. Though the front of the shop opened onto Main Street, the back of the shop seemed miles away. That's how it is in Utopia.

A canopy of oak limbs shaded most of the half-acre yard. Well-manicured St. Augustine grass covered the ground, with the exception of one circular patch of sand. This patch was about six feet in diameter. In the center of the sand was a buried coffee can, similar in size to a golf hole.

The men headed for the sand. The coffee can held large metal washers typically used to secure huge nuts and bolts on various kinds of machinery. These galvanized metal discs had a hole in the center and were about three inches in diameter. As I observed the men taking washers from the cup, I realized that some sort of game was about to begin. And I was the pigeon.

Johnny had a smile on his face as he let me in on the game before us. "This is a great game for putting," he began. "It is a game of distance control first and accuracy second. It's an offshoot of 'washers,' which is a common game of the cowboy in these parts. We'll play this for a little while then head to the golf course for a real putting contest. As you'll soon discover, this game is great for improving your putting. We do this several times a week when things are slow."

Johnny reached for a few washers. As he was warming up, he explained the rules of the game. "The man pitching throws from behind each of five stakes in the ground. The stakes are set at five feet, ten feet, twenty feet, thirty feet, and forty feet from the coffee can. Each man gets five pitches during his turn."

I watched as Johnny pitched from each spot. He stood motionless facing the cup as he prepared to pitch. His eyes were riveted on the target. He then allowed his arm to swing underhanded freely from the shoulder joint, straight back and straight through. Everything else remained motionless.

I learned that when pitching washers, unlike pitching horseshoes, the feet never move. The physical movement and objective were very similar to putting.

Johnny sank a washer from five and ten feet. The other three tosses from the other distances surrounded the hole but failed to drop; his accuracy was uncanny.

Johnny picked up a few washers while dodging the other guys' throws. He handed me several.

"Here's the catch," he said. "The scorekeeper keeps track of money earned. If a person makes it from five feet, everyone pays him a dollar. Two dollars for a make from ten feet. Three dollars from twenty feet; four from thirty feet; and five from forty feet. Here's the fun part: When it's your turn, you can choose from where you want to pitch. You have five pitches. You obviously have a better chance of making it from five feet, but you make a lot more money from forty. Not only is it a game of distance and accuracy, it's a game of risk-reward.

"Oh, one other thing: The money doubles after each round. The stakes rise quickly. Everyone starts with forty dollars. Once you have spent your forty plus any overage you might owe at that point, you are eliminated. The game continues for five rounds or until someone has all the money."

I was beginning to get the picture. I was in a game of skill with guys who had been doing this for years. I figured that it was enough like putting that I would be able to hold my own once I got the hang of it. Even if I were to lose some money on their court, I knew I could earn it back later when they entered my court at the golf course.

"Hey, tour pro," Jake called out to me with a smirk on his face, "You takin' good care of my money?"

I found out quickly that these particular cowboys were trash talkers. While they weren't vindictive, their chatter never ceased. If you had thin skin or rabbit ears, you were in serious trouble.

As I was about to take my first practice pitch, I could feel all eyes upon me. My first attempt was two feet long from the ten-foot stake. I tossed again with the same result. My next toss was one foot short. Finally, on my fourth toss I got the range but missed wide right. My fifth toss hit dead center, to a few whoops from the crowd.

"Let's get started," Jake yelled with authority. "Guests first," he said as he attempted to hand me a set of five washers.

"I defer," I said, buying a little time to observe and learn. And so the game began.

One cowboy pitched while the scorekeeper, Justin, kept tabs. The cowboy named Chuck made two from ten feet then moved back to thirty. He missed twice but hit on his fifth and final pitch. He gave a good fist punch in the air with a loud yelp.

"Luck!" yelled Jake. "I got ten bucks that says you can't make it from thirty on your next turn."

"I'll take it," grinned Chuck as the side bets were off and running.

"Can I have a little of that, too?" asked Duane, whose nickname was ATM. He got this nickname from winning so often that the others had to head for the ATM machine.

Chuck just nodded to the scorekeeper, making it a done deal.

Johnny put his arm around my shoulder and whispered in my ear, "The side bets are where the real game is played with these guys. Hang onto your wallet, and don't let the big bass get to your emotions." He said this to remind me of the lesson I had learned down at the river a couple of days before.

Jake took a turn. He immediately moved to the twenty-foot stake and dropped two in a row. This guy was amazing. He moved back to forty to the delight of the gallery.

"Here, you're gonna need these," joked Justin as he attempted to hand him his glasses. "I got ten to five you don't get one within six inches."

"You're on," he said excitedly as he pitched to about ten inches short.

"Come on, granny, can't you get it there?" asked ATM. Jake just looked at ATM and said, "Talk is cheap when you don't have any skin in the game. I only have two left. You want the ten-to-five deal?"

ATM nodded to Justin to make note.

Jake took aim and let it fly. It bounced off the cup and spun to about a foot. He had one pitch left. Just before he let it go, he balked. He looked right at me and said, "You want the ten-to-five deal? I'm down to one pitch."

Despite what Johnny had just told me, I was caught off guard. Thinking I had a sure deal, and to keep from looking like a coward, I nodded to Justin.

ATM slapped me on the back with approval, and the chatter intensified as Jake focused in on the target. He let it fly. The washer landed two inches from the cup and bounced up on the lip where it teetered for a moment then fell into the bottom of the cup.

Jake looked to Justin and said, "Cha ching."

Justin gave an accounting of Jake's turn: "That's $16 from the three side betters and $11 from the rest of us for a total take of $81."

The game was barely under way, and I was $24 down.

It was my turn. I started with a couple from ten feet, missing both. I chose to move back to twenty feet for my final three shots. While my direction was good, my distance control was off, missing each of them long or short.

By the time the first round was over, I was down $30. Early in the second round I lost the remainder of my $40 and was therefore the first to be eliminated from the game. The game was to end when one person had all the cash or five rounds were complete.

I watched in amazement at the talent these guys had for a simple game for simple folks. I also watched and learned as they remained focused despite the trash-talking and mounting pressure. Johnny was the second to be eliminated. He walked over and stood next to me as we leaned up against the oak tree.

"You can learn a lot about putting from watching these guys pitch washers," Johnny whispered. "My entire philosophy of putting has changed since meeting these guys. The genesis of new thought often happens in the simple things of life."

He then asked me, "What can you learn about putting from these cowboys?"

As the game continued I began to throw out several thoughts. "They're confident. They're focused despite the chatter. Their rhythm never changes."

"Good start," Johnny said with a nod. "What about their misses? Do you notice anything about their misses?"

Watching intently I began to see a pattern. They missed a little left or right but hardly ever missed long or short. Their distance control was exceptional.

"They have the distance down," I replied. "They seldom miss long or short."

"Precisely," Johnny exclaimed. "They have a great feel for distance. It amazes me to this day."

He continued, "You know what I have noticed in putting through the years? All good putters have great distance control. There are two variables in putting: distance and direction. Most people over-focus on direction and under-feel distance while putting. In washers, distance is paramount. You don't have to read the break, and most people can pitch fairly straight, so the game becomes one of distance control. That is why it's a great game for putting improvement."

Johnny motioned for me to watch Jake's technique. He was

about to pitch from thirty feet. "Where are his eyes focused? What part of his body moves? Is his pitching motion a straight line or circular like a golf swing?" Johnny quizzed.

Jake faced the target with both eyes looking at the cup. His arm hung freely at his side. The pitching motion was straight back and straight through with no manipulation needed to produce this perfect pendulum movement from his shoulder joint. His body remained perfectly still, as if chiseled in marble.

"He is looking at the hole with both eyes, his arm is the only thing that moves, and because he is face-on to the target, his arm is free to swing in a straight line," I responded.

Johnny picked up a stick that was about four feet long. He gripped the stick near the top with his left hand, placing his left thumb on top of the stick. He placed his right hand down the stick about two feet, holding the stick between his thumb and index finger. He moved the bottom of the stick just outside his right foot so that his right arm hung freely from his shoulder joint. He anchored his left arm against his chest with his left hand placed just in front of his right shoulder joint so that the stick was perfectly perpendicular to the ground. He stood naturally, looking with both eyes at the cup. He then moved his right arm in the exact motion the cowboys were using to pitch washers. The stick swung straight back and straight through effortlessly.

"If a person had never seen anyone putt, and you taught them to putt this way, do you think it would work?" Johnny asked as he swung the stick back and forth as though he were putting.

Before I could answer, he said, "You're about to witness one of the great experiments in golf. None of these guys had held a golf club before I built the Links a few years ago. I had played washers with them for several years. Pitching washers with these guys gave me an idea for a new putting technique that is superior to any other

I have studied. You are about to see what putting looks like with binocular vision, one moving joint, and a perfect pendulum motion that moves freely in a straight line from an uninhibited shoulder joint."

The washer game ended after three rounds with ATM collecting all the money. The cowboys looked to Johnny to see if he was ready to head to the course.

Johnny responded, "Let's reload our guns with cash and head to the Links."

With this, each man approached ATM who served as a human cash register, handing out dollar bills from his winnings in exchange for twenties.

On the way to the Links, Johnny made a profound statement: "I respect tradition, but I have a passion for truth."

He paused to let me reflect, then continued. "The purpose of golf is to get the ball in the hole in the least amount of strokes possible. As long as you use conforming equipment, it doesn't matter what the stroke looks like."

"In each generation there are innovators who rise up and challenge tradition. Take golf equipment, for example. Innovators have had a lasting impact in our generation with new materials such as titanium and designs such as the expanded sweet spot. Long-standing techniques have also been challenged in recent years, especially in putting. The long putter and belly putter have emerged along with the claw grip, split grip, and left hand low."

Johnny took a right off the highway onto the one-lane road leading to the Links. He looked at me with that twinkle in his eyes and said, "You are about to witness the future of putting. I call it face-on putting."

"These cowboys started with a blank slate. On that slate I taught them to putt looking at the hole with binocular vision while using their familiar washer pitching motion. From a physics standpoint, they have several advantages over tradition. Binocular vision allows a truer picture of the target and line. They have one moving joint instead of two. They use the shoulder joint in such a way that it swings the club in a straight line like a pendulum with absolute freedom. Unlike traditional putting, the putter is anchored at the top. And finally, their feel is focused in one hand instead of two. Can you imagine Monet painting with two hands on the brush?"

My imagination was piqued. Johnny pulled into the parking lot and turned off the engine. He glanced at me before opening his door. "If you think those guys were good at washers, you haven't seen anything yet. I'm telling you ahead of time: Hang on to your money."

The cowboys headed to the practice green. All of them owned the same unusual looking long putter; not a traditional putter in the group. Not a golf shoe in the bunch either, just cowboy boots. They tossed their balls on the green and began to talk trash while putting in the manner Johnny described. I had never seen anything like it. I had never let my imagination run wild enough to try something this unorthodox.

Tradition has a vice grip on most people in general, and golf is a game where tradition is sacred. I was beginning to realize that it had a grip on me as well. It would take a player of monumental courage and confidence to break ranks this dramatically. Yet these guys knew no difference. To them they were setting tradition, and common sense ruled.

I reached in my bag for my putter, forgetting that I had broken it at the tournament on Sunday. Johnny said that there were some putters for sale inside the pro shop that I could borrow. Entering the small shop I saw both traditional putters and custom made Face-On putters that Johnny had helped design. This was the putter each of the cowboys was using. I hesitated just for a moment but decided since there was money on the line, I would stick with a traditional short putter.

I headed out to the green to warm up. It was the first time in my life where my traditional side-on style was completely out of place. The cowboys just smiled because in their hearts they knew that their common sense face-on style would hold up against my experience. They also knew that they could play upon my self-consciousness.

I caught myself watching with intrigue. These guys were good, I mean really good. Who would have believed that a bunch of local cowboys could become such accomplished putters in such a short amount of time?

As I observed, I realized what they were doing actually made much more sense than my two-handed traditional style. Golf is one of the few sports where we don't look at the target while performing. We play to a memory. But these guys were looking right at the hole while putting. It seemed to me that a true picture was more powerful than a memory. Not only that, I reasoned that looking with both eyes, binocular vision, was superior to my side-on method, where my eyes were not the same distance to the hole. Their putter faces were plenty big and face-balanced, allowing them to putt comfortably while looking at the hole. I also noticed how freely their shoulder joint moved. Their putting arm hung freely from the shoulder allowing them to grip the putter between the thumb and other fingers, the same way a violinist would hold a bow or an artist a brush. And freedom is the key to putting. Because their left hand anchored the top of the putter, they putted with one hand focusing all of the feel in the tips of the fingers, the place in the body where the sensory system congregates. Their left arms were anchored against their chests at a 45-degree angle with the left hand placed just in front of their right shoulder joint. The arm anchored in this fashion allowed for a perfect hinge.

Before the game began, I had a sense that I was the pigeon once again, about to be taken for more money.

The game was explained to me through great interruptions and trash-talking. It was the same as before. We would putt to holes of five feet, ten feet, twenty feet, thirty feet, and forty feet. Each person had five balls each time and could putt to any of the holes he chose. Each make paid the same as before. Only makes counted.

I had never witnessed so many made putts in my life. These guys were all good. I was most impressed by their distance control. The feel from washers transferred to the green. Looking at the hole seemed to give them a more direct access to feel. When their putts failed to go in, they just missed slightly to the left or right. What remained were tap-ins. In a real game of golf this would essentially eliminate the three-putt.

During one of my turns, I was challenged to use the face-on style. They said if I would, they would double my fee for makes. I was in the thick of the race for the money, so this was a ploy to distract me, I was sure. But it was also a chance to be a hero and to try something new. I accepted their challenge and, without practice, immediately made two from five feet then one from ten. I then chose the thirty-foot putt for my last two putts. The first missed but the second one dropped as did the mouths of the cowboys. I collected my money, which more than made up for my deficit for the day, then quietly stepped to the side of the green at the prompting of Johnny.

"Four out of five ain't bad," he said. "Think you could have done that with your side-on style?"

I was speechless because of the ease of the method. As I thought back to the putts, one thing really stuck out: It was simple.

"That was amazing, wasn't it?" I replied. "You know, I didn't have one technical thought in my head. I just looked and let my arm swing."

"Think you would ever use that in a tournament?" he asked.

I wanted to say "Yes," but I feared change. Especially one that was this different. I was one of those who grew up respecting tradition, especially the deep traditions of golf. I knew putting wasn't my strong point, but I had practiced for years to get to my current level. My mind was racing. Quitting now would relegate all that practice to waste, wouldn't it? Surely today was a fluke. It couldn't be that easy, could it? This was Utopia. What about the real world of competition. And even if it did work, what would people think? I would be laughed at, gawked at, and never taken seriously. I would be consumed with self-consciousness. I could only imagine the doubt that would hound each missed putt.

The truth was that I was comfortable with what I had. Comfort zones are just that — comfortable. And so is tradition. It is safe, a great place to hide. But it is also the enemy of innovation and the destroyer of new thought. It can hold back the wisdom of creativity and squelch the dreams of man. And in the long run, it could conceivably steal talent.

Johnny could sense that he had just struck a nerve. Being a perceptive teacher, he knew that this was a teachable moment. So he walked over to the cowboys who were engrossed in their game.

"Hey, guys, we're done," he said, winking at them to let them know they had done their job well. "We're going to take a walk." They seemed happy, knowing they could have lost their shirts if I had continued to putt with this unearthed potential. In silence, we began our walk.

As we headed down the trail leading to the river, Johnny paused, as he often did before sharing a piece of wisdom, and pulled a piece of long stem grass to chew on.

"I think I know," he started. "I have been thinking about this for a long time, but I think I know."

"Know what," I asked.

"I know how putting technique got derailed. It had to have started from day one. You see, the object of the game was to hit the ball far, and to hit it towards a target. To hit the ball with any force, old Tom Morris had to approach the ball side-on so he could create torque. It takes torque to hit the ball with velocity."

I nodded in agreement.

Johnny continued, "They got so into hitting the ball across the fields that they stayed in the same position once they approached the hole. They no longer needed torque, yet they were used to approaching the ball side-on, so they continued in that manner."

Johnny reached in his pocket and handed me his keys. He then backed away about ten feet and asked me to toss the keys to his outstretched hand. Instinctively, I turned my body towards his hand and face-on, looking at his hand, tossed the keys underhanded, hitting the mark.

"There is a gold mine of truth in what you just did," he said as he returned the keys to his pocket. "Since you didn't need torque, you tossed the keys face-on. And instead of looking at the keys you looked at the target."

"Here's the point," he emphasized. "If putting had been invented before the game of golf, I believe people would have approached it just like the free throw, darts, or bowling." He mimicked each task as he spoke.

"They would have come at it face-on using the full power of binocular vision as well as a free shoulder joint that swings in a straight line. Secondly, I think they would have created a putter head large enough that they wouldn't have to look at the ball while putting. Today's oversize putters allow this to happen."

Upon reaching the river, we each took a seat on a large rock a few feet from the water's edge. This was the same place that I had learned to fly fish just a few days before.

Johnny continued his physics lesson, "No one would shoot a free throw side-on. The body just doesn't work well from that angle. The shoulder joint would cause the arm to move in a circle rather than a straight line. In golf, the swing moves in a circle from the side-on approach. That is why timing is so critical. It is no different in traditional side-on putting. Unless you manipulate your arms dramatically, there is no way to take the putter head back and through on a perfect line. However, when you approach from a face-on position, the shoulder joint hangs in such a way that a straight back and through motion is natural and free."

"I also believe the eyes are critical in this equation," he spoke as he tossed a rock toward a stump in the river. "Looking at the target has to be better than hitting to a memory, and binocular vision has to be superior to side-on vision."

"Finally," he added as he picked up a small stick about the size of a paintbrush, holding it in his hand as if he were about to paint, "nothing of great feel is done without the tip of the index finger leading the way. An artist, a surgeon, a violinist, they all use the index finger to lead the way. When we point, taste, tie, sew, or write we engage the index finger. Furthermore, we seldom use both hands when precision is needed. We focus our feel to one hand, and to the index finger specifically, with the thumb adding stability."

He looked at me with a sense of knowing in his voice. And with the confidence that came from years of golf instruction and the wisdom gained from working the land, he simply said, "This is the future of putting. In this case, tradition has sold us short and everyone, it seems, is captive."

His gaze continued looking right at me, staring all the way to my heart as if he saw something in me I had never seen. "Someone is going to lead the revolution. It just might be you."

Johnny stood up holding a flat rock in his hand. I couldn't help but notice that he held it between his thumb and index finger. He stood with the sun behind him, casting rays of light from around his head as he skipped the rock across the water. "Who would have thought a rock could skip, or metal float, or a plane fly?" he pondered.

He turned to me, "Is it tradition you seek, or truth?" he asked. "Is it excellence, or acceptance?" he challenged. "These are the questions of greatness. These are the questions that must be answered if a man is going to lead a revolution."

Johnny headed up the trail. "I'll see you at the driving range at eight tomorrow," he called back over his shoulder as he disappeared around the bend, leaving a potential revolutionary contemplating his future.

7. PILOT'S CHECKLIST

On Friday, the fifth day of my journey, I met Johnny at the driving range. He had told me that today would be focused on specialty shots. I was looking forward to what he had up his sleeve. I knew it would be creative. I just hadn't prepared for how creative it was to be.

Johnny drove up in his pickup, windows rolled down with the faint sounds of country-and-western music escaping from the cab. He motioned for me to join him, so I jumped into the passenger side.

"Before we hit any balls I want to take you for a ride," he said as we headed toward the back of his ranch, far from the golf course.

The ranch was quite large, about a thousand acres, and the roads were too bumpy to be in a hurry. Maybe the pace of life is relative to the roads we choose to drive. Whereas good roads may quicken our step to our next destination, Gandhi once said, "There is more to life than increasing its speed." Out here the cowboys moved to the pace life gave them. This week had been a time for recalibrating my internal metronome to that of the cowboys.

"Well, what have you learned so far?" he asked as we killed time along the way. Thinking back over the days, I began to pull together the pieces. "I've learned the importance of conviction in my method. My first day of reflection and writing under the oak tree made me see that. I have learned that rhythm, balance, and patience define my game. Fly fishing revealed my emotional tendencies and taught me how to take control rather than being controlled. I've learned about the art of the game and how important it is to take the time to picture a masterpiece. And yesterday I learned that truth is more important than tradition. I guess those are the things that stand out. My thoughts about the game have really been altered. I can't wait to try them out on the course."

"Well, if today goes well, we'll head to the course tomorrow," he said. "But today is the critical piece of the puzzle."

"What are we going to do way back here in the middle of nowhere?" I asked quizzically.

"You'll see soon enough," he responded. "How about helping me with this gate?"

The truck came to a stop at a big red wooden gate. I jumped out and opened it while Johnny drove through. I got back in the truck, and we pull into a cleared, level section of land. It was obvious that this long, narrow strip of grassland had been cleared very purposefully. We drove down the middle of the field in the ankle-high grass. It was fairly smooth, revealing that all the rocks had been removed. At the opposite end of this quarter-mile clearing stood a barn-looking structure with an old-fashioned wind sock atop the roof.

Johnny pulled up to the side of the building and killed the engine. "Watch for snakes," he said with a smile on his face. "They like to hang out in the shade of the hangar."

He swung open one of the two side-by-side barn doors. Inside sat a 1970s model Cessna 172 airplane. I opened the other door, and together we pulled out the plane.

"When I said we were going for a ride, this is what I meant," he said with a wry up-to-no-good smile on his face. "You have any objection to going up for a spin?"

Before I could answer he motioned for me to join him as he walked around the plane carefully, completing an external flight check. Constantly the teacher, Johnny said that the most important part of safe flying comes from disciplined flight checks. "By discipline and by the law you must conduct both an external and internal flight check, leaving nothing to chance," he said, seeming to have a deeper purpose in his exhortation.

Once he had checked the engine oil and fuel level and kicked the tires for good measure, we climbed into the cramped cockpit. I loved being in the plane. Just as I'd dreamed of being a fly fisherman, I had once longed to be a pilot. But golf had stolen this and most of my other dreams along the way.

The instruments and gadgets were fascinating as well as intimidating to a first time co-pilot. Johnny opened up his window and yelled, "Clear," as if there were anyone within miles of us. It was obvious that this man was serious about process. He then pressed the starter and the engine fired up with an initial puff of smoke, shaking and vibrating the little plane.

Johnny put on his Ray-Bans and handed me a clipboard. He asked me to read the Cessna checklist out loud, one item at a time. Once he had addressed the command he said, "Check." There were no short-cuts to this process. Johnny was as serious as I had seen him as he attended to this check list. You could tell this was the foundation of the flight for him. He simply was not going to engage the flight until the foundations were set.

We taxied out to the end of the level clearing, what I now

understood to be the runway. Johnny looked at me and said, "We have to hit a specialty shot on a runway like this. It's a short field with a lot of grass so we need to get the plane up as quickly as possible. Kind of like a flop shot in golf. Let's give full flaps, pull hard back on the steering column, and give it full throttle getting the front wheel off as quickly as possible. You like that idea?"

Acting like I had a clue, I said, "Roger."

Johnny pointed toward the tattered pink wind sock with a concerned look. "The wind in our face is our helper, but it is quartering from the left. This will be tricky with the short-field tactic. With all the wind we will be forcing under the wings, the plane will want to blow off the runway to the right. We'll have to be assertive and focused."

And with that vote of confidence he gave full throttle while standing on the brakes, wanting every bit of momentum in our favor once we initiated take-off. The noise was deafening at first. He let off the brakes, and with a jolt we rattled down the runway. Johnny pulled hard on the steering column. We bumped along, picking up speed. The front wheel lifted, and it felt like we were pulling a wheelie down the runway. Johnny was looking out the side window now, since the front window was pointed straight upward. I could feel the wind buffet us to the right while Johnny fought it back on course with a hard left rudder in a way that was calm yet aggressive. Finally the plane lifted. The wind quickly pushed the plane right. Johnny pushed the left rudder a little more, turned the steering column slightly left. We climbed out parallel to the runway, though from the ground it looked like we were dog-walking.

What a site to see. The Sabinal River snaked through the valley, cutting a swath through the majestic red cypress that defined the river. The hills rolled on for miles. The colorful native wildflowers dotted the landscape. I could see entire fields of bluebonnets, spring's gift to the pastures of Texas. It was as though I were riding shotgun with Robert Redford in the movie *Out of Africa* as he flew his biplane above the Serengeti. The sweeping rhythm of the movie's soundtrack was playing in my mind.

After a while Johnny's voice interrupted my movie scene. "To fly," he said, "is to focus. You start with an external walk-around checklist, ending with a look at the engine. Second, you enter the cockpit and go through the internal pre-flight checklist. These two checklists guarantee that the plane is airworthy. Confidence builds for the flight as you eliminate possible problems before you get airborne. Finally, you check the wind, plan a strategy, and focus. After all of that preparation, it is time to perform. With an assertive mindset and a calm heart and steady hand, you initiate the plan. At that point it is all feel; you move with the wind and bumps. You simply must feel."

He paused a moment to let the idea sink in, and then he finished, "It's a whole lot like golf. In fact it is identical to golf."

He climbed to two thousand feet. "Would you like a flying lesson?" he asked.

Before I could answer he told me how he had learned to fly. "After we moved to Utopia, I started flying. I got into it so much several years ago that I got certified as an instructor. I taught both my girls how to fly. I have taught a cowboy or two how to fly, including a few rodeo cowboys. They like to go up on hot summer days because it is like riding a bull when the plane is buffeted by all the heat currents."

Now I knew I was in Utopia. This was too good to be true. "Would I like a lesson?" I said almost in disbelief. "I have dreamed about this my entire life."

"Your feet control direction with the rudder. The steering column controls the wings and pitch," he began. "To turn, push one foot and turn the steering column in that direction. To go up or down, push or pull. Have fun."

Over the next hour I became familiar with the controls and felt as though I could fly if I needed to. Johnny, as usual, provided encouraging advice and made me feel like a Blue Angels pilot.

And then the fun came to a screeching halt. We were at about two thousand feet when Johnny reached down and turned off the engine. Everything went silent. "OK, we have an emergency!" he yelled. "We have to put the plane down somewhere! There is no time to get to the runway. Keep the nose down; keep the wings level. Where are you going to put the plane down?" he asked with great urgency.

I had signed on for flying lessons, but found out quickly I was getting crashing lessons instead. "What about the highway?" I said with a panicked voice.

"You can't land a plane on a road. There are cars and trucks and power lines. Get to a field," he said. "Keep the nose down, keep the wings level, and stay calm."

"What about that field?" I asked, hoping that I had made a good choice.

"You see those specks on the ground? Those are cows and goats. You can't land on cows. Find another field and hurry! We are losing altitude fast!" he exclaimed.

All of the sudden the stall warning went off and the plane began to buffet. "Get the nose down!" he said as he helped me shove the steering column forward until we were staring almost straight down.

There in front of us was a field full of crops. We were at one thousand feet by now. "How about that field? There are no cows that I can see," I say, almost begging.

"That is a good field; it's a corn field. Are you going to land with the rows or against the rows?" he asked, looking right at me.

I was thinking to myself, "What the heck kind of question is that?"

Seeing my incredulousness, he said, "We have to land with the rows. If you land against the rows, the plane will flip."

We headed toward the field at a steep incline. Until now Johnny had left me in complete control. At five hundred feet he said, "Well what do you know? The key has been turned off."

He turned the key and started the engine. It started right up, as if this were a common occurrence on a flight with Johnny. He grabbed the controls and ascended to two thousand feet. He looked right at me and said, "Son?"

"Yes, sir." I replied, my heart still racing and sweat beading across my forehead.

"As your flight instructor, by law I could never sign you off to solo a plane or take passengers up with you until you were ready for an emergency. To fly a plane with confidence is to know you are prepared for any challenge, any emergency. Up here is serious business. If you were my student, we would practice every conceivable emergency for a minimum of forty hours in the air before I would let you put your life on the line. Do you understand?"

I had never thought of it that way. Flying would never be enjoyable unless you had supreme confidence that you could solve a crisis in the air.

Johnny spoke with great authority as he shifted his focus to my golf game. "At your level of play in golf, it is no different. As your teacher, I will never sign you off to play in a tournament until I know you are prepared for the emergencies. And that's what today is all about."

I sat in silence. Johnny knew that silence was a great teacher. As

I stared out at the lush and beautiful landscape I began to understand a new truth. I knew for certain that I had never been properly prepared for tournament play. I had always played with fear, the fear of "what if." And every round was composed of a number of "what if's." That was the nature of the game.

As we headed back to the runway, we could tell that the wind had picked up a bit. We circled the field and saw the windsock had shifted even more from the left, blowing almost perpendicular to the runway.

"This will be tricky, but I believe we can do it," he said.

We approached the runway with half flaps instead of full because of the crosswind. The plane was aimed left of the runway, yet the wind effect kept us perfectly centered for the approach. Everything was going smoothly until just before touchdown. As Johnny was pulling back on the throttle and holding the nose off the ground, we were hit from the left by a gust. The right wing went low, the plane was blown off course, and in a split second we were in an emergency situation with the tip of the wing dangerously close to the ground.

In a blur, Johnny gave the engine full power, leveled the wings, and turned into the wind. Immediately he was in control, climbing the plane out for a go-around. It appeared that this was second nature for him. Had I been the pilot, I am sure we would have crashed.

We went around and came in with no flaps, slipping the plane down at a steeper angle. This time we hit the ground without incident, the nose quickly pushed forward, and the brakes quickly applied. We taxied in with plenty of room to spare. Johnny had a now-familiar look on his face, one that meant he was about to share a profound point.

"Many years ago my flight instructor turned off the engine during my first flight as well. He also told me the same thing I told you today. And it's times like this that I am eternally grateful. I knew exactly what I would do when I was hit by a crosswind during a landing. That is why we are sitting here now instead of in a heap of ashes."

We went through a shut-down checklist and killed the engine. Johnny's expression had changed. As we pushed the plane back into the hangar there was an urgency in his voice. "Confidence is supreme in this game. Confidence comes from being prepared for an emergency."

We jumped into the pickup and headed back to the range. My mind was flooded with new thought. Intense experiences do that to a person. I knew the importance of preparation. Shoot, I grew up with the Hogan mystique. I thought I could out-practice anyone. I loved to hit balls; I could spend hours on the range in the blistering Texas sun, thinking I was in paradise. I had memorized John Wooden's famous quote, "Failing to prepare meant preparing to fail." Inside I finally began to see that game day was about preparation, not only for the swing, but for the environment ripe with emergencies. I had a new template, a new perspective and I knew that I had failed to completely prepare in the past. I had not had the mind-set of preparing for the emergencies.

Back at the range Johnny spent the remainder of the day connecting the dots between flying and golfing. Practicing for the emergencies meant an overhaul in my understanding of preparation. Johnny explained that golf is the worst practiced sport in existence. He helped me understand that hitting balls from a perfectly level lie on nicely manicured grass, one ball after another with the same club to the same target with no ramifications is not golf. He said that in all other sports scrimmaging was the best form of practice. In golf, that meant getting on the course or creating a setting with course-like lies and obstacles.

"Before we hit a shot, we need to develop a pilot's checklist for tournament play. Earlier today, the checklist gave us confidence that the plane was airworthy, and the emergency checklist helped me avert a crash. I want you to listen to me carefully. Your pre-shot checklist will become the most valuable asset in tournament play. It will be your foundation. From this day forward you simply cannot afford to hit a shot without a commitment to your pre-shot routine. It will become your security system.

"Going through the pre-flight earlier today gave me complete confidence that the plane was airworthy. When it was time to take off, I was able to focus my attention on the feel of the takeoff, handling the crosswind and currents with the movements of my feet and hands. Takeoff is an art. The conditions are never the same, and the pilot must be free to feel and respond to the conditions."

Johnny continued, "In golf there are five major checkpoints leading to the club head's initial move off the ball. First is the observation check. This includes such things as the wind, lie of the ball, elevation change, distance, and obstacles. If a player misses any of these, the shot is already compromised. Second is the strategy check. This includes choosing the target, club, and type of shot. If a player misses any of these, the shot is compromised. These two checks are similar to the external and internal flight checks we did this morning that guaranteed that the plane was airworthy. In golf, the decisions have been made by this point. It is time for athleticism to take over. A couple of days ago we defined this next stage as art. Art has three components, remember?"

Remembering back to the shot from beneath the great oak, I responded, "See, feel, and trust."

"Precisely," he agreed. "This is not only your takeoff mind-set, it is also your response to emergencies. In the plane the overarching emergency response is always to level the wings, give full power, and turn into the wind. In golf it is to see your shot, feel the shot, and trust it. While this doesn't guarantee success, it gives you the highest probability to reach your fullest potential. And that, my friend, is all we can ask of ourselves. Before each shot you will go through this routine. Your response to any emergency such as a poor shot, bad lie, bad break, or any other distraction is to move your focus to your checklist. Your checklist is your security system."

We started at the range with the nine basic shots in golf: low hook, normal hook, high hook, low straight, normal straight, high straight, low slice, normal slice, high slice. Johnny lined up nine balls then called the shot. I had five seconds to pull it off. In five seconds I had just enough time to see, feel, and trust. We did this for the better part of two hours.

In the beginning I was just saying the words. But as Johnny coached, I began to live the words. I would see the shot, I would deeply feel the shot, and I would trust or let go. The feeling was amazing the first time I really lived each word. When I said, "See it," I remembered the painting from behind the big oak and could see the shape and trajectory. When I said, "Feel it," my mind clicked into the words that defined my fly-fishing method on day two. Rhythm, balance, and patience moved from my head out through my body. When I said, "Trust it," I signed the masterpiece. I knew that I would never go back and that I had just learned the true secret of the game. How simple, yet how profound. I understood for the first time how all the pieces of Johnny's unorthodox teaching were coming together. It was brilliant.

For specialty shots, Johnny believed you should never change the swing. Instead he advocated adjusting ball position, stance, and opening or closing the club face as the most efficient and effective ways to success. He taught me that manipulating the ball with these pre-swing adjustments was much easier than attempting a different swing for each of the nine shots. These adjustments, he said, would free me up to always have the same swing, rhythm, and thought process during the swing. He would not allow overs. If I missed the shot, we moved on, just like golf.

We moved to an area he had designed near the range and practiced the five basic lies. Flat, uphill, downhill, ball above my feet, ball below my feet. He kept me moving between them, never allowing me to be lulled into rote memory practice. He kept my mind moving, and challenged my creativity on each shot. Eventually I hit each of the nine basic shots from each of the five basic lies. And each time I was committed to the see it, feel it, trust it routine.

We then moved to the rough and practiced bare lies, normal lies, shallow lies, and deep lies. We experimented with each club with each lie to see how it would react. I took notes so that I would have a better understanding of strategy from the rough. The most revealing shot from the rough was with the metal woods and hybrids. They seemed to part the grass with ease. Johnny showed how opening the face with a seven- or five-wood produced an array of shots that would serve me well.

Every once in a while Johnny would throw a tree in the way. I had to hit it under and around both ways, and over the top, experimenting with various clubs until I understood where my odds were.

Next, we practiced various lies around the green and I was amazed once again at the versatility of the utility woods around the green from the rough. They were literally choke-proof because of their ability to part rather than catch the grass.

As the day ended, I felt like Chuck Yeager, the great test pilot. I had hit more types of shots on this day than any other day in my life. I had hit each of these shots with a see it, feel it, trust it checklist. I learned a tremendous lesson. In practicing for the emergencies of the game, my confidence grew. I felt more prepared for the real game of golf than any previous day of practice in my life.

The day of practice ended with Johnny saying, "Now I will sign you off to solo the plane."

I knew what he meant. I was ready for the emergencies of tournament golf. He pulled out his pocket knife and cut off the back of my shirt. This, I learned, was standard procedure for every pilot who solos for the first time. But I felt sure they weren't wearing an expensive golf shirt at the time.

8. HICKORY STICKS

O n day six, I drove down the one-lane entrance to the Links
that had become so familiar this life-altering week. It was a
"windows down" sort of road. You wanted to experience it, not just
drive it. Unlike the entrances to the modern-day master-planned
communities and country clubs, this stretch of road was flanked by
the authenticity of life. Nothing was imported. Without the help of
a gardener, native wildflowers bloomed in concert with the natural grasses and vines. Sensing their short-lived splendor, wildflowers sprang to life with a flurry and lived life greatly, knowing the
slower-growing grasses would survive them in the coming heat.
Cattle stared you down with curiosity while chewing their cud,
oblivious to the world outside of their fence. The century-old rusted
barbed-wire fence served its purpose faithfully, held together by the
stoic rot-proof cedar posts born in the valley. Obsessed by failure
earlier in the week, I had been too preoccupied to experience life
beyond the surface, missing what Monet lived to paint.

The lane eventually gave way to the pothole-laden parking lot
shared by both the cemetery and golf course. I imagined the lot

occasionally served both patrons grieving the loss of a loved one and those bereaved over failing once again to close the deal on the inward nine. I could attest that the line sometimes blurs between three-putting the eighteenth and losing a distant relative. The game had an insidious way of clouding a man's perspective.

As I stepped out of the car, the smell of freshly mown Bermuda grass hung heavily in the air. This sweet fragrance brought thousands of memories to mind. The smell is intoxicating to all who play the game, an opiate accompanied by eternal hope. Each time a golfer steps to the first tee surrounded by this tantalizing fragrance, he stands at even par. We all own par on the first tee. Hope is eternal. It's on the 18th green that one has to face the music. How similar to life! A parking lot serving both a cemetery and golf course seemed only appropriate.

I had come so far since my last round, a forgettable saga to be sure. Though it wounded my pride, my will was still intact. Golfers who rely on pride will eventually tuck their tails and look for a game that is less revealing.

I was chomping at the bit to test the new me. But I can't say that I had great excitement for playing this course. Though I looked forward to my time with Johnny, I was a little embarrassed for him as I surveyed the layout. This was, in the truest sense of the word, a minimalist nine-holer. I wondered who would actually pay to play here. The only way my friends would play this track would be with a case of Lone Star longnecks in tow. It truly was a goat ranch.

The small crowned tee boxes looked like large sea turtles strewn across the landscape. With each rainstorm, erosion had softened the edges of the once rectangular surfaces. These tiny teeing areas were as exhausted as the worn ground beneath a swing set. The clay-based fairways were crisscrossed with cracks wide enough to swallow a ball, the product of hot summers and an inefficient watering system. The grass was a competition between Bermuda and crabgrass, with the latter holding the upper hand. The predictable back-to-front sloped greens were small and shaggy, evidence of a mower that was constantly on the blocks. There was no bunkering to be seen. Most of the small water hazards were as dry as a west Texas oil well. My motivation for playing here was about as enthusiastic as going to a chick flick on a blind date gone bad.

Johnny came out of the salt box pro shop with the screen door clapping behind him. He waved hello then reached down and swung across his broad shoulders a well-worn, old-fashioned canvas golf bag. As I reached into the trunk for my clubs, he said that I wouldn't need them today. He motioned for me to come on over.

Confused, I asked Johnny why I wouldn't need my clubs. Johnny said, "Today we're going to visit both the roots and the future of the game. We're going to join with the pioneers of the game who played with hickory shafts, wrapped leather grips, and small persimmon woods. We're also going to visit the future of the game with this Face-On putter. Today we'll culminate the week with this new challenge."

We were off to the first tee. I found out later that Johnny was the purveyor of the new state Hickory Shaft Open held in the early spring at the Links of Utopia.

For a moment, I considered leaving. I couldn't imagine the absurdity of playing a lousy course with clubs that time had passed by. To make things worse, looking into the bag, I saw only seven clubs. Six ugly rusted ranch implements and one out-of-place long putter. I could only imagine how bad the hickory shafted clubs would feel and how short I would hit them. Furthermore, I was sure they would ruin my swing and that I would embarrass myself in the process. How could shooting ninety and not hitting the ball out of my shadow give me a boost in confidence?

But I caught myself and stopped short. Johnny's creativity had challenged me each day. Should today be any different? As we walked past the cemetery on the way to the first tee, I could sense an eerie comradeship with a few souls inside the picket fence. Just maybe they wielded a similar hickory stick many years ago.

The first tee box, due to erosion was only about ten feet wide. "Nothing like an uneven lie on a tee box," I thought to myself. Cracks ran the length of the box because of the poor clay soil and perpetual drought in this part of the country.

Johnny handed me a scorecard. My task, he said, was to keep two scores on the card. The first was the same as always, my outcome score. The second was called my concentration score. It represented the number of shots on the hole that I went through my routine, my pilot's checklist. See it, feel it, trust it. This seemed easy enough, though I was to discover it was challenging, especially with these implements.

"The reason for the concentration score," Johnny explained, "is for accountability to the process. People say they are going to change, but without accountability, they seldom do."

"The goal is to have the two scores match at the end of the day," he said. "I don't have a lot of guarantees, but you can take this to the bank. If you commit to your check-list, you increase your probabilities for success."

The first hole was a 380-yard slight dogleg to the left. I teed the ball, ready to play. "At least I can use a modern ball," I thought to myself.

"By the way," Johnny said, reaching into the bag, "I want you to use this old balata ball. It is softer and easier on the antiques."

I caught the used ball as he tossed it to me. I hadn't seen one of those for several years. It was an old Pro-Trajectory, slightly yellowed with age.

I re-teed as Johnny reviewed the process he wanted to see. I moved aside as he stepped behind the ball to physically demonstrate the routine. "Start by calling your shot. Target, shape, trajectory. Remember, you are an artist. You have to paint it before you can sign it."

He moved into the shot. "Next, approach the ball setting the clubface to the target. Look to the target, saying, 'See it.'"

Johnny paused for emphasis, looking at me. "It is important that this is a look, not a glance. Remember, we are hitting to a memory. A look sees the shot; a glance does little more than see direction. Without a look, there is no memory; and we revert to mechanics, an inferior method at best. Think of the look as a gunfighter look. A confident, unhurried look. Not only will this cement the picture, it puts you in an aggressive frame of mind. A glance is skittish, revealing hope rather than assuredness."

I thought of how I had spent a good portion of my career taking quick glances once I approached a shot. Johnny was right: Often I was just trying to get the shot over with so I could see the outcome. I was hoping for something good to happen and felt an urgency inside, rather than a confident, settled feeling. I liked the idea of the gunfighter stare. It fit the attitude I desperately needed.

His eyes moved back to the shot as he continued to demonstrate the routine. "Look to the ball, waggle the club, and say, 'Feel it,' as you look back to the target. This feel stage should capture the essence of your game. Remember the words you discovered on Monday. Rhythm, balance, patience, freedom. These are the words that are your ticket to feel. They are your internal compass. They must come alive with these clubs, or you will suffer the consequences. Finally, as your eyes return to the ball, say, 'Trust it,' as you initiate your swing with absolute freedom."

Johnny then caught me completely by surprise. He took the club back with one of the sweetest backswings I have ever seen. It was long and flowing, perfectly in balance, with a slight pause at the top. His downswing was art, poetry, and music harmonizing like a Dan Fogelberg chorus. This old man was a player.

Now it was my turn. While I had done this flawlessly on the range, doing it on the course with hickory sticks would require another level of focus. This was the test.

"Son," he implored, "you have a choice. You can see this as a waste of time, an amusement park activity. Or you can trust me and the process I have chosen. If you choose to trust me and let yourself enjoy this game, you just may see greatness unfold. It is your choice. You see, I believe greatness is revealed in the unorthodoxy of life. It is in thinking out of the box labeled 'comfort zone' that we discover truth. Our box is nothing but a self-imposed prison, a trap set for unsuspecting souls. My passion in life is to set people free from their boxes."

With that he put his arm around my shoulder. We turned slightly, allowing us to survey the entirety of the minimalist course, taking in his little corner of the world. He took a deep breath as if smelling the opiate of hope. His eyes twinkled with contentment and glistened in the sunlight. He glanced at me, and with the artistry of a great poet whispered, "There are no boxes in a place called Utopia."

Once again his words cut to my heart. As a child learning the game, I had been free and uninhibited. Days were filled with wonder and shot-making adventures. Learning was ever-present and a three-putt was just that. A score was a goal, not a definition of a man's self-worth. Every swing adjustment began with "uncomfortable" and "inconsistent" as companions. Yet breakthroughs always followed, nipping at their heels. But with performance expectations and the posting of scores, it became too costly to my performance identity to accept being uncomfortable and inconsistent as stepping stones to improvement. This is where my childlike adventure ended and my building of the prison began, where passion and love for the game gave way to an emerging fear of failure. It is the point along the journey where the ordinary take leave en masse, leaving only the silhouetted faces of the courageous aboard a train to destiny. Maybe that was the true brilliance of Mozart, the child prodigy who historians tell us never quite fit the box of adulthood.

Like a bully, posting a score intimidated the learning process. Our culture of immediate gratification appreciates only today's performance, not tomorrow's promise. We base our identity and self-worth on the shallow opinions of scoreboard watchers and on the empty meaning of the number posted.

I can see now, after many years, that when I accepted my comfort zone the colors of life began to fade. In the words of Don McLean's classic song, "It was the day the music died." It was an insidious time in my life when I began to believe the lie shouting from the scoreboard. I was a prisoner, and Johnny was my defense attorney seeking an appeal.

As the game was about to begin, Johnny jolted me from my thoughts. "How do you normally mark your ball for a tournament?" he asked.

"I put three red dots along the seam on both sides."

"How common," he mused. "I want you to try something new today. Print SFT instead of the three dots. Each time you look at your ball, it will coach you. Your mark will become an integral part of the process rather than a common practice used for identification only."

"Here is one more thing I want you to use," he said as he flipped me a pewter coin. "Mark your ball on the green with this."

The coin had SFT on one side and Utopia on the other.

Johnny handed me the driver. "You have got to be kidding me," I thought to myself.

The grip was slick and pencil thin. The small pear-shaped persimmon head paled in size to the modern titanium giants. It appeared to have at least 12 degrees of loft. The shaft was fairly stiff with a little play toward the hozzle. It was shorter and heavier than my driver.

A choice was staring me in the face. Complain and be a bad sport or try to get into it. Thus far the week had been magical, so I figured this method had potential. The choice was made.

I made a few swings with the club. There was an accompanying whoosh that added an audible sensation to the swing, an extra rhythm check missing in today's aerodynamically engineered equipment. The driver didn't feel as foreign as I'd expected. I recalled some old films I had seen of a young Bobby Jones and other golf legends swinging with similar clubs. The image was of rhythm and balance with a long, flowing swing. The words I had discovered on Monday continued to come into play.

I stood behind the ball and called for a slight fade with a low trajectory aimed down the left center of the generous fairway. Unless a fairway had significant bend to the left, I always opted for the Hogan power fade. I walked up to the ball and aligned the club to the target and took my stance. As I looked at the target, I said, "See it." I looked down at the ball to connect with it while dancing a little with my feet and waggling the club. I'm sure this club, born in a time of elegant dancing, was waiting to see if I would lead or follow, dance or count steps. I looked back up at the target and said the words, "Feel it." I could sense the rhythm, balance, and patience of Bobby Jones as I settled in for the shot. As my eyes returned to the ball, I said the words, "Trust it." And it was time to dance, a dance in which I was not the leader.

The ancient club moved off the ball like a willow branch in a summer breeze. It was as if the clarinet lead in Glen Miller's "Moonlight Serenade" coursed through my body. In that instant, I realized I had entered an old place, a place of my childhood — a place without walls or inhibition, a place of art, the curator of freedom.

Staying in perfect balance with patience at the top of the swing, my body coiled like a screen door against the spring's energy, only to close with the progressive momentum of a slamming door. It was as though I had been born with this club in my hand. The sound at impact was significantly different from a titanium driver, but the feel of the ball coming off the face was as sweet as any homer I had hit in Little League.

Finding the sweet spot is akin to finding religion or the taste of an aged cabernet. I was reminded in that split second of the root attraction of the game. It's the sweet spot. That's what keeps us coming back. There is no sensation in life quite like it. The sweet spot is an addictive force.

The ball flew off the face with unanticipated force and traced an arc of a liberal fade. I was surprised at the distance of the shot. While I lost about 20 percent in distance, the ball still traveled a good 240 yards. I was impressed. The grooved and rounded face proved to shape the ball more noticeably than my straight-faced modern driver. Being a shot-maker at heart, my intrigue was engaged. My imagination was further captured as I noticed the club maker's name on the face. "Sweet Spot" was etched into the rich persimmon, revealing that the club maker understood. I felt a connection to this pioneer in club design.

As we walked to the ball, Johnny reminded me once again of the goal. "That shot was well executed. But I don't care about the outcome of the shots today. I am only interested in the input, period. Looked to me like your checklist was flawless. Good job."

The seven clubs consisted of two woods, three irons, a wedge, and a putter. I found my ball about 150 yards out. Johnny said that the irons were similar to a three, five, and seven, subtracting about 10 percent for distance. I normally hit a seven about 170 yards, so I chose it, figuring the 10 percent should get me in the ball park. I called for a slight fade, knowing that I would need the ball to sit softly to stay on the tiny green.

The well-worn grip revealed that this club had had a full life. I wondered to myself if it had ever been gripped by a pro, if it had ever contributed to a tournament victory. As I looked down at the rusty old blade, I was shocked at the thin profile. There was no question that perimeter weighting was a foreign thought at the birth of this toe-heavy design. The sweet spot on the irons was sure to be the size of a dime.

Once again the checklist dictated my approach. As if at the keyboard on a computer, I entered the data: see, feel, and trust. As before, the sound the club made was unfamiliar, but the feel was pure. The ball reacted like a knock-down nine, taking a long first hop before reaching the green. It came to rest about fifteen feet beyond the hole, leaving a slow downhiller, an oxymoron at most golf venues.

Johnny handed me the long putter as we reached the green. I had thought deeply about what Johnny had said two days ago. Maybe this was the future of putting. I was open to trying it out; after all, putting had been the least consistent part of my game. Using my new SFT coin, I marked the ball, wiping off the accumulated moisture from the dew-laden green.

The putt read downhill with a slight break to the left. I replaced the ball and took a couple of practice strokes while looking face-on at the hole. I tried to calculate how hard I must hit this putt since the head of the putter seemed a little lighter than mine. I thought of how slow the green must be, yet it went downhill. My head was full of calculations as I stood over the putt. The putter moved back as my mind said, "The putter is light, the green is wet, the grass is long. Make sure to hit it harder than would seem necessary."

With that great inner coaching, I put a little extra effort into the hit to make sure the ball would get to the hole. It rocketed off the face of the putter, failing to take the break, and ran past the hole a good six feet. "A terrible putt," I said to myself.

Johnny seemed to be amused as he stood with his hand on his chin, those steely eyes of wisdom waiting for my reaction. Uncomfortable with the silence, I let my mouth run.

"Caught all of that one, didn't I? I guess it's going to take a few holes to figure out the pace of the greens and to get used to the future of putting," I blurted out in my defense.

"Bravo, bravo," Johnny sarcastically bellowed. "You play the victim well. Excellent acting, great blaming, bravo, bravo," he said as he paused for effect. "You just reverted to an also-ran, a wannabe, one of the myriad who will remain ordinary; and it only took three shots."

I wanted to crawl into a hole and hide. I wanted to be miles from this place. It was only minutes ago that I thought this was going to be a special day. What a wimp I was!

"Before you beat yourself up, which has no value or place in this game," he said, cutting my self-pity off at the pass, "let's just look at the truth.

"I have one simple question. What is our one goal today?"

I thought back to our conversation on the tee. Johnny's challenge to me was to focus on the process, the checklist. Our goal was simple: stay with the process on each shot.

I replied, "It's to commit to the checklist on each shot. See, feel, and trust."

"Did you?" he asked calmly.

"I felt as if I needed to adjust my feel, since these were unfamiliar greens and this was an unfamiliar club," I began. "So I focused on calculating feel rather than going through the checklist. To be honest, instinct took over and I just forgot the checklist."

"Instinct? Don't you mean intellect? You see, what we are after is indeed instinct. What you did is trump instinct with calculations. Your intellect, your need for control, and your fear of failing took over. The truth is, you didn't believe enough in your instincts to let them take over. That's all. You didn't hit a bad putt. You hit the exact putt you calculated. You aren't a bad putter and this isn't a difficult method. You're a bad chooser. You chose intellect over feel. You are back to counting steps instead of dancing. It is inferior at your level. Can you see?"

"I hear what you are saying, my heart says you're right, but my mind is trained to take over. How can I change?" I pleaded.

"You have the answer. You tell me," he returned.

"Commit to the checklist." I answered and then continued, "Can it really be that simple?"

"Simple is relative," he said. "Simple in concept, difficult in practice. But you have the answer to that as well. If you take the challenge and keep track of your progress on the scorecard you will have dialed in to the surefire way to stay accountable. Let's finish the hole, and I will demonstrate."

I still had a six-footer, uphill, with a little break to the right. This time I was committed to letting go and seeing what would happen. I let go of all excuses, including the newness of the method and the length of the grass. I simply observed and sensed.

I let the genius of my eyes and mind compute. Something clicked, maybe for the first time in my life. It was the idea of "let." I am not sure I had ever truly let go during a scoring round in my life. I had lived a life of control on the course. Maybe on the range I let go a little, but I can't say it was a habit. Control was always nearby.

It was as if a light switch had been turned on in a long-forgotten room. It was the room of sensation, a room where all the senses lived. Intellect hid them there long ago, afraid that they would undermine order and structure. There was too much on the line to let go; it would be irresponsible not to work at it and make it happen.

By letting, I could sense the speed and break. My body absorbed the information and did the work for me, bypassing, for all practical purposes, intellect. I moved into my checklist. I said, "See it," and traced an image from ball to the hole. I said, "Feel it," and sensed the perfect stroke needed to make the putt I saw happen. I said, "Trust it," and let the putter head move. The putt happened. It wasn't forced or controlled. It wasn't coerced. There was no wishing or hoping involved.

The putt responded perfectly and fell to the bottom of the hole. In that one putt, I realized that a putt is a sensation, nothing more. Intellect could never do what sensation just produced. Furthermore, intellect could never describe the sweet spot; it can only be sensed.

Johnny could tell that a light had just come on. I could see him trying to hide his wry smile as he turned and walked towards the next tee box.

"Write down your two scores before we think about this next hole," he coached as I climbed up on the turtle back known as the second tee box.

I wrote down a four for the score and a three for the process. I failed to go through the process on the first putt.

"You can do better than 75 percent," he said as he handed me the driver. "You have 100 percent control of the process. It is all about mental toughness. Let's see what you're made of."

I looked at the hole before me. It was the hole of the great oak, the one we painted on Wednesday. The hole was about 380 yards long. Trees lined the left side. The right was open all the way to the huge oak, which lay about 270 yards from the tee. My strategy was to keep the ball down the left side to avoid the tree, which stretched its arms across the entire right rough and one-fourth of the fairway.

The wind was blowing left to right about 15 mph. Since I normally played a fade, I would be challenged, especially since the trees lined the left side. I would have to play a controlled draw that leaned back into the left-to-right wind.

I chose my target and called my shot from behind the ball. I walked into the shot and set my club to the target. As I looked out to the target, I said the word "see." As I looked back to the ball and made a waggle, I felt the sensation of perfect timing and tempo along with a slightly in-to-out swing. I looked back to the target and held my focus with an aggressive posture as I said the word "feel." As my eyes returned to the ball, I whispered the word "trust" as the club moved off the ball with no hesitation. I let my body work and once again sensed the essence of the game.

The shot began as planned, but the wind overcame the lean of the draw. On its descent the ball began to drift to the right slightly. It hit the center of the rock-hard fairway and bounded forward and hard to the right. It came to rest about twenty yards behind the oak on the right side of the fairway.

Johnny let out a chuckle and said, "The oak is a champion at getting the first-time player. That's why we held art class there on Wednesday."

Changing the subject, he asked, as he headed for the ball, "Did you accomplish your purpose on that shot?"

I was about to say "No," because I failed to hit my target. But I was learning that his simple questions were deceiving. I thought about my purpose. It was to go through my process on every shot, which I did.

As I handed Johnny the driver, I said, "Yes." He looked pleased as he asked what I was going to do next.

I said with an air of confidence, "Enjoy the walk in Utopia, enjoy our conversation, and look forward to the next shot."

Without missing a step Johnny said, "You're good, son, you're really good."

I could tell that he knew that I knew and that my life was indeed changing. My golfing mind had been reborn. I was a different person from the empty shell of a man that had shown up on Sunday evening.

He continued, "Remember, the checklist puts you into position to hit the best shot at any given time. It doesn't guarantee perfection. It just increases your odds for hitting the shot you picture. You always want the odds in your favor. Once you have done that, react and move on." He slapped me on the back and said, "You are well on your way to greatness. Be expectant."

"Here's a thought for you that will serve you well on your journey." He proceeded to share one of his many simple but profound quotes: "Always set an extra place at the dinner table, so when destiny comes knocking at your door you invite him in as though you have been expecting him."

Johnny had a way with words. He also had a way with timing. In the silence of the next twenty seconds as we walked to the ball, this quote sunk deep, touching and inspiring the source of greatness, a seed that had been sown earlier in my life but had failed to be watered. It was a seed born out of childhood stories of valor and heroism, knights in shining armor, and warriors riding upon white horses. The hero was always prepared. When his number was called, with much confidence and skill he struck down his foe with great expectation of victory. In my heart of hearts I wanted to be one of them. But somewhere along the way, I slammed this door, hearing only the voice that said, "You are ordinary; extraordinary is only for the books." But this week a story was being written, and expectations were increasing.

As we approached the ball, my thoughts returned to the round in front of me. I had indeed enjoyed the conversation between shots.

It was about ten feet left of the site of my "masterpiece." I swear this man was a genius or a prophet. The jury is still out on which. How in the world could he have anticipated this?

My mind returned to the painting and the shot I hit on Wednesday. The only difference was that I was in the fairway, there was a little more wind, and I didn't have my clubs. The five-iron in this set looked to have more loft, so I went with the three-iron, called a mid-iron by the club maker. It looked and felt like a four-iron. I would just have to trust it. "Novel thought," I thought to myself.

Once I chose the club, I stood behind the ball and called my shot. I saw a low slice under and around the tree taking a few hops then running up on the green. I could see the red shot line from the painting all the way to the pin set in the back right. I approached the ball and set the club. The top line of this club was also razor thin, an anomaly in today's market. I looked to the target and said the word "see" as I took a waggle. I looked to the ball and adjusted my feet, keeping them dynamic through my routine. I looked to the target and repeated the word "feel." I remembered the sensation of the word "let" on the previous putt. I let the painting of Wednesday emerge; I let the shot cover me; I simply let go and let instinct take over. I returned my eyes to the ball as I said the word "trust," allowing the shot to happen.

The shot came off low and sliced to the right. It flew under the limbs about sixty-five yards out, spinning to the right and catching a little grass to halt its momentum. It rolled up on the fringe, slowing as it headed for the pin. For a moment it looked as if it were really going in. It trickled just past the hole, leaving six feet for birdie.

"Picasso!" I thought to myself.

Johnny responded by asking, "Is that piece of art for sale? I would like to hang it over the mantel." He continued with a smile, "I want to buy your art before the public catches on and I can't afford it.

"By the way," he taught, "the only thing more powerful than calling your shot is recalling a shot. What you just did is recall the shot from Wednesday. Always savor your shots, so you can take advantage of this most powerful tool in your armor, the recall."

He handed me the Face-On putter as I walked to the green, feeling as if I were in Never Never Land. I had never felt these sensations on the course. And furthermore, I was using ancient tools to produce uncanny results. I could sense that this was no ordinary day. I could also sense Johnny was no ordinary man. He found a way to unlock hidden treasure, release latent talent, and water forgotten seeds of expectation.

I thought philosophically for a moment. Don't we all need a Johnny in our lives? Where are all the Johnnies? Have we run them off, choosing instead band-aid cures and swing gadgets, slick technology and the flavor of the month swing guru? In a larger sense, where have the Johnnies gone in our world? We teach to the test in education. We hire new employees only to throw them to the wolves. We hold organizations sacred and leave it all on the court for these meaningless entities, yet the hearts of men and women remain imprisoned for the lack of wisdom being shared. Where is wisdom these days? Who is teaching wisdom? I never had a course in it, but this week my life had been altered because of it. I thought of the multitude of unsung heroes that seek to teach wisdom in the small forgotten communities, the true Utopias of the land. Maybe that is why cowboy poetry is capturing the imagination of so many these days.

Johnny could sense the questions inside. He could see the pieces coming together in his student. In his heart he knew that his purpose was being met. He was a rancher at heart, and ranchers know about seed seasons. When a seed is sown in the right season, its yield is great. Johnny was watching his crop with much anticipation.

Without speaking a word, he grabbed the flag and moved out of the way. I watched him carefully as he walked away. I was in awe of a man who would give a stranger a week of his time and a lifetime of wisdom. Finally I turned to the ball. I let the face-on method enter and take root. I assumed the identity of a great putter. Because of wisdom shared, the seed of revolution had been planted. I didn't know when, but I did know that I would indeed unveil this method in a tournament some day. In the meantime, my putt hit dead center, and we walked to the next tee, where I wrote down two scores.

Art continued to unfold hole after hole. Words became fewer and fewer between us, for all the teaching had transferred. An epic was under way, and the force of wisdom, combined with latent talent, brought out a storyline for the ages. When the sun was setting beyond the falling of the final putt, I'd set a course record. While I stayed in the present over each shot, the irony was that I did it with the help of ancient hickory, trees felled over one hundred years ago, and by embracing the future of putting. But the hero of the day was wisdom. A forgotten tool passed from one generation to the next on an ordinary day in an extraordinary place called the Links of Utopia.

As I leaned against my car while changing shoes, passion for my future returned. I was impressed with my round and the extraordinary happenings of the week. I had come here desperate for hope, and it had been given. I had been desperate for answers to golf's most baffling challenges, and I found them. I had been in need of a mentor, and he showed up. With tears in my eyes, I thanked Johnny for all he had given. Knowing my time with him was done, I asked, "What do I owe?" After all, what else could he teach me? I had just set a record with antique clubs on a course I had never seen just one week after my worst defeat.

"Son," he said with a look of someone hiding a great secret, "here, this Face-On putter is for you. Destiny will knock when it is time to unveil it in tournament play. And secondly, I said seven days, not six. I will see you here in the cemetery at daybreak for our final lesson."

He fired up his tractor and headed for home, leaving me looking into the cemetery at sunset and wondering what tomorrow would bring.

9. BURIED LIES

The next morning as the sun was peaking over the horizon, I checked out of the Utopia on the River Lodge. It had become a sanctuary for me at the end of each day. I spent several hours during the past week walking and reflecting along the Sabinal River beneath the century-old cypress trees. The absence of a phone and the solitude became a blessing. I had somehow been led to this place at a critical juncture in my life. I headed north to the Waresville turnoff. Driving up the one-lane road my mind was full of anticipation. How could anything top off my round yesterday? The knowledge I received this week had changed how I felt about my career forever. What more could Johnny have to offer?

I pulled up to the cemetery and parked next to Johnny's tractor. Johnny had arrived sometime earlier. He was deep in thought, hardly noticing my arrival, as he moved slowly through the engraved granite epitaphs of those who had gone before us.

It was a small, well-kept cemetery, surrounded on three sides by a white picket fence and with an old, crumbling stone wall at the entrance. The cemetery was shaded by the arms of the valley's largest oaks. Though the journey of life for some had ended here, I felt a great sense of security in this place.

Johnny motioned for me to come in. His hand was wrapped in a blood-stained red bandanna. He said that he had cut it while moving some rocks earlier in the morning. I could see fresh dirt on the other hand, revealing that a rancher's work was never done, even on the morning of the Sabbath. I soon would find out the nature of his work on this Sabbath.

He drew my attention to one of the headstones. The epitaph read, "Though he never earned a degree, he was wise. Though he never left the Sabinal valley, he impacted the world. Though he died young, in Christ he lives." We walked past several others that simply had faceless names devoid of comments, with two dates separated by a dash. He stopped and pointed to another. The dates on the stone read April 10, 1901 — June 7, 1901. The epitaph read, "Like a spring bluebonnet in the valley, our precious April bloomed in glorious splendor. She was chosen for heaven's bouquet after a brief but fragrant stay in the garden of Utopia." I thought what it must have been like to lose a child. I looked down and shuffled the grass with the soles of my shoes, my heart heavy. Then I trudged slowly after Johnny.

Finally, Johnny knelt before what looked like the oldest and smallest stone in the cemetery. He took off his hat and used it to dust off the engraving. "This is my favorite," he said. The moisture in his eyes glistened in the early-morning sunlight as he read out loud, "1875 – 1941, My Daddy." We both stared at the two words for several minutes. This man's entire life was defined for us in these two simple words. I felt privileged to be in the presence of this grave. There was something in these words that moved both of us to the core.

I noticed that a new grave had been dug near the picket fence on the side next to the driving range. There was fresh dirt on the shovel, which was leaning against a nearby tree next to an unfinished headstone. I could see only one date etched in the natural river rock chosen to serve as a reminder to the world of this person's life. The unfinished date etched in the stone was 1979 – . I asked Johnny if he knew anything about the impending funeral. He said that it was for a young friend of his who was relatively new to the valley. The funeral would be later in the day.

Johnny quietly walked over to the largest tree beside which was a small box. He sat down at the base of this mighty oak. The two seemed like brothers in so many ways. I followed. We sat for a moment in silence. Though no one was around, I felt like we had an audience. I picked up several acorns, squeezing them in my hand to relieve a little tension.

Johnny reached inside his worn Levi's jacket and pulled from the inner pocket a small, leather-bound book. It was worn and well-read. As he held that book in his bandaged and dirt-stained hands, he paused and asked me a simple question: "What will your epitaph say?"

I looked up quickly, dropping the acorns from my fingers. Johnny stared at me with those piercing but compassionate eyes. I looked away from his gaze to the many graves that surrounded us. I thought of the words from the several headstones we had just read.

My young life flashed before my eyes. My thoughts were consumed for the most part by golf. After all, golf is what I did. It defined me to the point that my golf score and self-identity had merged into one.

As I thought back to the question, I started to say something like, "He made it big on the PGA Tour," or "He won the US Open." But before the words came out, I realized how shallow and insignificant they were in a place like this. Out of nowhere, his question had tapped into a deep well of passion of which I had been unaware. I wanted my future headstone to say something profound. When people in the future read it, I wanted them to be moved. I wanted to be remembered for something other than golf, but for what? I realized I wouldn't have any say in the matter; those left behind would write the epitaph according to the life I had lived.

Johnny knew that I was struggling. He could see clearly that my life had little in the way of foundations. I had simply become a golf score. If my life continued on this course my epitaph might read, "Played to a plus three in golf, but had a thirty-six handicap in life."

Before I could answer, he led me down another path by asking, "Why did you feel so great after yesterday's course record?"

I replied that it was an example of my true potential and how hard work could pay off. I said that it felt great to see shots fly so true and putts find their mark time and again, especially with the hickory clubs and a new putting method. I continued by saying that I was finally in control of my game again.

Johnny stopped me before I went any further. "While that all may be true, I believe you used yesterday's fine round to validate yourself as a person." He continued, "You said that you had never felt so good about yourself as you did when you completed that round. Wasn't it just a week ago that you were devastated by a golf score?"

There was a pause for reflection for both of us. "Son," he said, "you are well on your way to living a life controlled by a score. Let me let you in on a little secret. Life in the end will be measured by significance, not a golf score. Significance will be defined by your character, relationships, values, virtues, and faith, not by a golf score. The book I am holding reveals that we will all stand before our Maker someday and give an account of our life. It goes on to say that all the insignificant wood, hay, and stubble of our lives will be consumed by fire, revealing the significant costly metal and precious stones that remain unscathed by fire. It looks to me like you are well on your way to a bonfire of insignificance."

The instrument panel of my life was going haywire. What I thought to be true north was about to let me down. I had stayed in Utopia for a week for a checkup, yet I was receiving a heart transplant. My life was being overhauled. I knew what he was saying was true, but I didn't know what to do about it. I had always believed that my calling in life was to be a golfer. I was finding out that I had sold myself short, that I could do more. The morning light was breaking through the limbs of the oak. A beam of sunlight shone directly on the black book in his hands. I could see a worn and faded cross on the binding, which revealed to me the contents. He reached his injured hand into another pocket for his reading glasses. Then he opened the Bible. He asked if I would be offended if he read a few verses from the Good Book. After all, he said that it was customary for the Bible to be read in a cemetery, especially on the day of a funeral.

I had never been much of a churchgoer, especially since I played golf on Sundays. But I remembered my grandmother's funeral and how I was comforted by the words of the Bible before we laid her to rest. So I nodded for him to continue.

Before he began reading, he looked directly at me and made this statement: "I am about to tell you about a man who lived many years ago, yet was at the same crossroads you are this morning. He was a performer who spent his life dreaming about the big win, the day he would be heralded as the best. He was defined by what he did, and his livelihood depended upon his performance. He was a passionate man, a contender. The only difference between you and him is that you are a golfer, and he was a fisherman. His name was Simon.

127

"When you showed up here earlier this week, you were devastated by a poor performance. You came by chance to my range, primed for listening and learning. In the story I am about to read to you, Simon had just fished all night but caught nothing. He was tired, hungry, and humiliated by his performance. While he was cleaning his nets near a crowd of people, he began to listen to the teacher Jesus, whom all the others had come to hear.

"Before I continue, you need to know something. While I am not a preacher, I believe with every fiber of my being that there is a God. It is almost impossible to look up at the starlit sky each night in the Utopia valley without being overwhelmed with the majesty of His creation. I have seen His handprint upon my life over and over and felt His presence closer than the wind upon my face. I also believe that He has a plan for my life and yours. I know that our meeting was not by chance.

"It is our job to seek God and listen to His calling for our lives. I believe that He sent you to me at this time in your life. You are an empty man on a journey to success, a destination that has never filled the deep longings of any man's life.

"You have been controlled by your performances in life and the opinions of others. You have lost sight of what it means to live a life of significance. You see, success is a destination while significance is an eternal calling.

"I believe in the words of this book. We call them the living words of God, because they change lives and give life where there was emptiness. We also call them living because they speak to each of us in a very personal and life-transforming way each time we open the pages. Because of this, the story that I am about to read you could affect you for eternity. It is up to you to listen or cast it aside. No one can make that choice but you. God gives us the grace to accept or reject Him. Eternity rests on this choice. It is the profound mystery of life."

Johnny asked if I were ready. My heart was racing. It's not easy being the only man in the pew. While my intellect told me to run, my heart pleaded to listen. It was starved for freedom from a prison of insignificance. I listened to my heart; after all, I am a feel player. He began to read from the book of Luke in chapter 5.

Simon had just finished an awful performance. He had fished all night and caught nothing. He was a talented professional whose livelihood and reputation depended largely on his ability to perform. While he was washing his nets of defeat in the early morning, he began to eavesdrop on the powerful words of a nearby teacher named Jesus. Soon Jesus stopped and looked directly at Simon, asking for his help. The people were crowding in so much that many could not hear him teach. He needed a better pulpit from which to teach so he asked to borrow Simon's boat. Simon agreed and paddled him out a little from the shore. Jesus continued to teach as the crowd listened intently.

After a while he concluded his teaching. He now turned his focus to Simon as the conversation became very personal between two men. Jesus offered up a direct challenge to Simon. Little did Simon know that this challenge would eventually change his life and alter the course of human history.

Johnny stopped for a moment to reflect out loud, "I don't believe that we take into consideration the far-reaching effects that our everyday decisions have on our destiny, the lives of others, or the world as a whole."

Johnny continued his reading. "Jesus looked Simon square in the eye and said, 'Push out into the deep waters and let down your net for a catch.' While all eyes of the crowd were on Simon, he felt the penetrating gaze of Jesus. What would he do?"

Johnny stopped again and began to conjecture. "I'm sure several things ran through Simon's mind. First, he might have reasoned that he was the fisherman and that he would know more about fishing and where the fish were than Jesus would. Second, the deep waters presented a significant risk to a small boat. Out there the storms come up at a moment's notice, the waves are big, and the winds are dangerous. Third, this was his boat; he was the captain. He always called the shots. What would it say to the people if he gave in, especially if he failed or got caught in a storm?"

Johnny said, "It is no different for you. The decision facing you is basically about who is the captain of your ship."

Johnny had slipped me into the story. Indeed, I was facing the same challenge as Simon.

Johnny continued with the story. "Simon answered the challenge by saying that he had competed hard all night and experienced great failure. In fact, hours of effort had ended in complete futility. Simon, in a move that probably surprised even himself, then said, 'However, because you asked, I will.'"

"It was an act of faith and obedience to the teacher," Johnny said with deep feeling. "Even though conventional wisdom frowned on taking the small vessel out into the deep, there was something about Jesus that stirred the heart of Simon. His teaching, his countenance, his personal challenge all moved Simon to trust. Little did he know that because the voice of the master came from within the boat, there was ultimately no risk involved in this venture. Jesus was going with him. The real risk was not to go."

Johnny continued, "Simon paddled out into the deep, a speck on the horizon for those on the shore. He then let down the nets and experienced something he had always dreamed of. He witnessed the greatest success of his career. The success was so overwhelming that he signaled to his partners to help with the catch. They caught so many fish that both boats began to sink."

Johnny mused, "Sounds like a course record to me, and with unconventional clubs, I might add."

After this interjection he continued teaching, "It was during this dream come true, at the moment of his greatest triumph, that a paradigm shift took place. Simon realized for the first time that he was in the presence of the author of success. This teacher was indeed who he said he was, the son of God.

"Simon's response was one of awe and fear as he fell to his knees among the mess of fish, sensing for the first time in his life that there was a God, and that he was in the boat with God's Son. When a person has that experience, the Bible says that the scales of unbelief begin to fall from their eyes, and they see for the first time the enormous chasm that exists between a Holy God and a sinful man. Initially, Simon was so overwhelmed that all he could do was beg the teacher to leave."

Johnny's voice cracked as he said, "It was then that Jesus reached out his hand to Simon and said, 'Don't be afraid.'

"Son," Johnny said as he cleared his throat, "have you ever been afraid? I have lived long enough to see tough men cry. I have seen champions tremble. I have seen way too many unbelievers face death alone. He is holding out his hand to you. Don't miss His grasp."

Johnny paused and wiped his brow with his blood-stained bandanna. He took a sip from his thermos, then continued. He lowered the Bible and looked at me with the seriousness of a surgeon with good news, "Not only was the teacher the author of success, He was and is the remover of fear. While life is tough and the prospects of dying someday even tougher; the teacher offered ultimate security in an insecure world. Then Jesus presented a call, which is the same to all of us; 'Follow me, and I will make you a fisher of men.'

"Jesus gave Simon the offer of a life of significance. Would he take the challenge? Would he follow the call? Or would he stay with the fish seeing them as the path to opportunity and fulfillment?"

Johnny closed the book. He looked at me and began to share his challenge to me. "When you showed up, you were devastated because of a game called golf, a game that had all the makings of your god. When you discovered new insights into the game this week, your talent was unleashed and you saw a glimpse of your true potential. When you experienced this new success, your body embraced it like a narcotic; you were on a high. The high, based on a golf score, would soon have worn away, possibly during the next round, maybe before. Like an alcoholic in need of a drink, you would spend the rest of your life trying to get a high from your score. Your life would be a series of ups and downs, a life consumed by the fear of failure. This consuming drive would hide God's true calling in your life, and you would be well on your way to a meaningless, powerless, and insignificant headstone.

"But the good news is that you are at a crossroads. You have the choice of taking a very different road. On this new road you leave the fear of failure in the dust. Your identity is not tied to a game but to God. You will find your purpose not in a game or score but in a calling that has eternal implications.

"The Bible states that this road leads to heaven, and that faith is the fuel that moves us from mile marker to mile marker. The first step is to realize that there is a God and that He is calling you to an adventure. The second step is to ask Him to forgive the sin that has kept you from this road in the past. The third step is to get in the boat with the Master, make Him the captain and push out into the deep waters. He will tell you where to fish. The outcome is in

His hands, not yours. The fear of failure will be removed from your performance. Success will no longer be the goal; significance in the process of fishing will hold all the emotions that you have longed for, namely peace, patience, and significance."

I was speechless. I could sense the truth. My heart was racing, "Open the prison door," but my mind was screaming, "How?"

Johnny's quiet, earnest voice broke my internal conversation. "I'm going to leave you alone with your thoughts. If you choose to go down this new road I want you to do something before you leave this place. Earlier in the week we worked on buried lies. I want you to revisit that lesson in a new way. Inside this box is a pencil and two pieces of paper. Write down the lies that you have learned along your journey in life, those lies that you have established in your heart even though the weight of them has been crushing your soul."

He watched me nod, then continued, "On the second piece of paper I want you to write the truths of God's Word that you have heard today. These truths will set you free and will establish a new calling in your life, one that will begin to rewrite the epitaph of your life."

He stood, dusted himself off, and tucked his Bible back into the inner pocket of his jacket. As he towered over me, he gave me a final task. "When you have finished that task, your week here will nearly be complete. I want you to take the buried lies you have written, put them in the box, and carry them over to the grave that has been prepared for this occasion. As you kneel next to the grave site, ask God to forgive you for running in the wrong direction. Ask that He lead you down this new road through faith in His Son. And tell Him that you are ready to follow Him as you give Him the helm of your boat.

"Once you have prayed, take the shovel next to the tree and fill in the hole, putting to death the old lies that propelled you toward a life of insignificance. The Bible says that a man must be born again and must become a new creation. I have already chiseled in your birthday. You take the hammer and chisel and add the date that you laid the old lies to rest and were born again. You can chisel an epitaph if you'd like. Place the stone on the grave as a reminder of your new life and follow God's lead as you leave this place."

Johnny must have seen the inner turmoil in my eyes. He gave me a strong bear hug, jumped up on his tractor, and said, "See it, feel it, trust it. See His face, feel His presence, and trust His love." He drove off, leaving me alone in the cemetery with an open grave.

I knew that I had a choice, that I was at a crossroads. The week began at a fork in the road and ended at another.

I knew he was right but the questions began to bombard my mind. What will everyone think? What if I do this and God isn't there? What if this has all been another psychological ploy just to get me to change?

Then I remembered his words, "This is a matter of faith." Faith to me had always meant to believe in something that you couldn't see. But when I contemplated this week, I could see evidence of God. Not only had I miraculously chosen to turn to Utopia at the fork in the road; I had met Johnny and had witnessed God in his life. Even more compelling, the words of the Bible came alive. The story of Simon was my story. I just hadn't gotten into the boat yet. I wondered if I would catch some fish if I moved out into the deep.

Like Simon, I took the challenge. I was tired of the empty road I had traveled. It was exhausting and devoid of meaning.

I slowly opened the box to find two pieces of paper, a pencil, and a small black Bible identical to Johnny's. I was surprised to see my name embossed on the cover. There was a note attached to the Bible that read, "I knew you would make the right choice. Once you have written down the truths, fold them up and put them in your Bible.

As you learn new truths, add to your list until you need a notebook to keep up with the blessings that God will shower upon you as you let down your nets for a catch."

I took the piece of paper and the pencil and began to search my heart for the buried lies. I found several:

1. My golf scores are a reflection of my self-worth.
2. Failure in golf is failure in life.
3. Success in golf will bring the fulfillment that I long for.
4. My calling in life is to play golf.
5. The opinions of others are paramount in the choices I make.
6. God is a crutch for the weak.
7. Tradition is sacred and never to be challenged.

I opened the box and placed the buried lies inside. I replaced the lid and carried the box toward the open grave. I now knew why Johnny's hand was bleeding; the blood-stained shovel handle revealed the grave digger's identity. I tossed the box of lies into the grave as the rustle of leaves and twinkle of sunlight applauded my action.

I knelt down. Feeling a bit awkward, I began a conversation with God. I asked His forgiveness for putting a game before Him and for seeking fulfillment on a road leading away from His calling. I thanked Him for His son, who gave His life for me. And then in a promise I thought I would never make, I gave up control of my life. By faith I handed over the reigns of my life. I pushed out into the deep.

I lifted my eyes to heaven. My face was caressed by the gentle Hill Country breeze. The fragrance of fresh-cut hay was like honey to my senses. The sun warmed my back as it streamed through the great oak's thick branches. I felt a peace deep in the longings of my parched soul. I experienced for the first time in my life the freedom that came from knowing the truth. Silence enveloped me. If only this moment could have lasted forever.

I could hear the voice of God whisper my name in the deafening silence. I noticed the true work of His artist's hand as I took in the landscape as a new creature. The scales fell off my eyes, revealing His handprint on everything I saw. A miracle was taking place, and it had nothing to do with a recovery shot to the green. The buried lies were being replaced by a flood of truth. It was like cool summer rains bringing life and hope where drought had ravaged the terrain. A transformation was taking place that cannot be put in words. A dry spring was beginning to flow.

The shovel stood against an oak, beckoning me to finish the job. As I touched the blood-stained handle, my knees buckled to the earth. Emotion overwhelmed me. Tears burst from my eyes as I thought of the two men who intercepted me along the road to insignificance. I thought of Johnny, whose blood was shed during the digging of this grave, a man who had followed his calling by investing in me this week. I also thought of the captain of my ship, the man who shed His blood for me on the cross so many years ago.

My shoulders were heaving, and I shed enough tears to fill the grave. I was so thankful. I was overwhelmed with the thought of how easy it would have been to miss this chance meeting. I could still see the sign at the fork in the road last Sunday. I chose Utopia because of the name but hoping for more. I was not disappointed. At the lowest point in my life, God led me to Utopia.

With every shovel of dirt tossed onto the box of lies, I felt a sense of freedom emerging. I couldn't shovel fast enough. I hardly noticed the blisters forming on my hands. I was done with the past and ready for a new beginning. Finally, out of breath, hands bleeding and drenched in sweat, I stamped down the dirt. It was time to chisel the headstone.

While hammering the second significant date of my life, I left more than a few pieces of my flesh upon the stone. This was a new task, with foreign tools. I saw these as wounds of passage. I thought long and hard about an epitaph that would be appropriate for my journey. Johnny's parting words loomed as the only choice. To rid the soul of buried lies, there is only one hope: "See His face, feel His presence, trust His love."

10. A NEW VOICE

Leaving the cemetery, I headed north toward Austin, the newest site of the PGA Tour's Texas Open. I am signed up for the Monday qualifier at Morris Williams, an old worn-out course that has hosted much of the history of golf in Texas. Affectionately named "Mo Willy," this course put the University of Texas golf team on the map.

Armed with a new perspective on life and a revamped mental game, I anticipated the round like a lion waking up hungry and ready to hunt. With no fear of failure, I headed in my car for a new destiny. There simply is no power in life like having the right competitive perspective coupled with a bullet-proof mental strategy. For the first time in my life, my compass was pointing to true north.

After checking into the Holiday Inn Express and having some barbeque at the County Line, I wrote a script for the next day's round. While the course was familiar, I wanted to be ready when the spikes went on. My script described two goals: Keep the game in perspective, and see it, feel it, and trust it on every shot.

I also stopped in the pro shop along the way and picked up a traditional short putter to go along with the Face-On putter Johnny had given me. While I knew I would putt face-on in the near future I would wait for the knock of destiny. In the meantime, I removed my two iron making room for both putters. I'm sure I was the only player in the tournament carrying two putters.

The Monday qualifier found me in a field of nearly 144 players. It seemed that every scratch golfer in Texas was chasing his dream this week. I continued to remind myself to play my own game. After all, Johnny said there is only one thing in golf that you control, and that is your thoughts. With my new confidence, I attacked the course from the first shot. There was no holding back.

With three early birdies I turned the front in three under. I knew that it was no time to play not to lose, so I continued to hunt rather than be hunted. On the back I was so focused on the mental routine that I lost track of my score, a state that I had seldom if ever achieved in my former life. In the scorers' tent I added up the numbers and checked them with my scorekeeper. This was the easiest 65 I ever shot. There were two 64's, leaving me the third spot of four. I was in the Texas Open!

There was no question that I was a new person. While every old instinct in my body wanted to fantasize about winning this tournament, the wisdom that I learned from Johnny fought back with a vengeance. I was committed to playing with a new purpose, one with eternal significance. I was pushing out into the deep and letting down my nets for a catch, and I knew that I wasn't doing it alone.

The field would be equalized this week, as the tournament had been moved from its original site in San Antonio to the new TPC course in Austin. Everyone would be playing it for the first time. I liked the way the course forced you to hit it each way and had plenty of risk-reward holes. I couldn't wait for the games to begin. While this tournament figured as one of the biggest of my life, I was supremely calm.

The first two days I was paired with Joe, a player known for his hot temper. I prepared for this distraction ahead of time in my script. He had no power over me or my focus unless I granted it to him. Following my game plan, I played two nice rounds of golf. Not many putts fell with my traditional putter, but I was patient, knowing it was just a matter of time. I also had been practicing the face-on method each evening in my motel room, knowing its time would come. My concentration score remained flawless, providing a great source of strength even as Joe went berserk several times, especially coming down the stretch. A crucial mistake on the final hole sealed his fate. I sensed that God had put him in my group as a reminder of where I had been headed. This guy was so wrapped up in his score and his failures that he had lost touch with his talent.

I experienced something else for the first time. I had compassion for him. I had never had compassion for a competitor before, especially one as explosive and rude as Joe. But something within my spirit saw through his rough exterior. I saw a lost and angry man. While he would never admit it, he desperately needed a friend.

I finished the two days at two under, making the cut by one. Eight-under was leading. After signing my card, I was instinctively about to head for the range. But something within my spirit led me in a different direction. Since Sunday, it seemed as though there was a new voice leading me, and I welcomed it. I instead headed for the parking lot to find my angry colleague.

I saw Joe standing behind an older-model sports car. I could tell that the car had a lot of miles on it. It reminded me of a car I had driven in college when my image needed the help of a certain kind of vehicle. When I reached him, he was slamming the trunk as if he hoped it would never open again. I didn't know what I was going to say. I had never approached a player in this kind of mindset before. There was a good chance that he might explode in anger at me. This was new territory for me; I was in the deep water.

With sincerity in my heart I simply said, "I know how you feel. Can I buy you dinner?"

Joe looked dumbfounded and said, "Yes." He said that he had already paid for his room for the night and didn't know what he was going to do next. We decided on a steak house and headed out in separate cars. It was the beginning of a new journey of significance for me.

During dinner Joe began to tell me his story, a privilege that I was to experience many more times in my new life. People all have stories; they just don't have many listeners. Thus the stories go unheard. I saw why he was so angry and explosive on the course. He had recently gone through a separation with his wife and two young children. A divorce was staring him in the face.

His wife couldn't tolerate his obsession with the game at the expense of his family. She and the children loved him deeply, but his ever-increasing moodiness caused an emotional roller coaster when he was home. They had begun to fear him. Not only had golf become his identity, it controlled his emotions, leaving his family estranged from the man they used to know and the man they desperately needed to love again.

Joe finished his story with tears in his eyes, revealing the pain that lurked just beyond the anger. He said he would like to change, but golf was all he knew. He didn't know how to harness its emotional grip. For an instant I hated golf for the devastation it had wreaked on this man's family. But I also knew the game was not to blame. Joe had to take responsibility, and, like us all, he needed a coach. He needed a coach with wisdom who wasn't too busy or preoccupied to share. Wasn't I just asking that question earlier in the week? Where had all the Johnnies gone?

We sat in silence for a minute. He broke the awkwardness by apologizing for ruining my evening. I immediately thanked him for the privilege of hearing his story. Then I asked him the question that Johnny had asked me only a few days earlier: "If you died today, what would your wife and kids write on your tombstone?"

Without hesitating, he said that they would probably leave it blank. "I have hurt them so much that they wouldn't know what to say."

"How does that make you feel?" I asked.

He answered, "My life is empty. That blank space on my tombstone would say it all. Golf just hasn't delivered."

My adrenaline was pumping as I felt this new-found tug inside my heart to share my story. He listened intently, his eyes never leaving mine. I knew the feeling; I had been in his shoes just a few days ago, desperate for hope.

After we finished our dinner and I had paid the check, we went to a nearby Wal-Mart, where Joe insisted on buying a shovel and a Bible. He was on a mission to bury the lies that were snuffing out his game and his marriage. His only thought was of seeking reconciliation, first with God and second with his wife and children.

I headed to my motel with the precious gift of significance flooding my heart. It was a high like I had never experienced. An eternal blessing had just flowed through my life for the first time. I had indeed become a Johnny. Even more amazing was that I was in the middle of a big tournament. But the tournament seemed distant and unimportant as I contemplated what had just happened. A family just might get their daddy back. How insignificant a golf score seemed!

11. DESTINY KNOCKS

Day three on the course was amazing. My ball striking was flawless. I played with rhythm, balance, and patience. There was freedom in my swing. All I knew was that my new mental routine seemed to keep me close to the zone. I never felt like I was more than a swing away from entering the zone. This new level of confidence allowed me to be patient, knowing a great round could break out at any time. That day it happened. I only needed twenty-six putts en route to a sixty-five, which left me a shot off the lead. I was at nine under. Two players were at ten. I would be playing in the next-to-last group in the Texas Open.

In the last group was Travis, who everyone referred to as the Lion. Nicknames seemed to follow greatness in this game. While he was still relatively young, Travis was sure to join the ranks of the King, Golden Bear, Shark, and Tiger.

Travis had a killer instinct and had left others in his dust for the past several years. Many believed that he would become the greatest player of them all. He capitalized on this media hype, causing many challengers to lose before the round began. For the first time in my life I would be contending with him in the last round of a tournament. But I had a very different perspective. I knew that it wasn't my calling to slay the lion, only to quell the myth.

The reporters were all over me. They had a theme and, like bulldogs, didn't want to let it go. It seemed that their only question was about my previous collapse and my inability to finish the deal. Not only did I blow it two weeks earlier in San Antonio, I had done it in a fashion they had never seen.

"How are you going to block it out?" they asked. Their incessant questioning forced me to rehash and experience the collapse of the century. My mind wanted to doubt, but my heart was now in control. There was a new voice in my life, and it was the voice of an advocate, not the enemy.

I smiled at the reporters and told them that the collapse was the beginning of the most significant experience in my life. I winked at them and ended the interview by telling them that I would reveal the rest of the story tomorrow on the winner's stand. I am sure it sounded arrogant. But my intention was to let them know that I fully expected to win and that tomorrow they would hear the full story. Now I had to deliver, and I couldn't wait. I was prepared for destiny to come knocking tomorrow.

Before the final round I was on the range, warming up. I was a little anxious and the adrenaline was pumping. It was wreaking havoc with my timing, thus my shot-making was a little shaky.

One of the officials approached and handed me a note. He said it was from a gentleman in the gallery. I opened it to find the message: "SFT." I looked around. Could he really be here? I looked carefully through the gallery but didn't see him anywhere. While I was in Utopia, Johnny made it clear that he had little interest in ever attending another PGA event.

My mind was racing, hoping he was here. I put the note in my pocket and returned my focus to my warm-up session. I immediately began to work on the feel part of my routine, focusing on rhythm and tempo. I felt the balance return to my swing. Focusing on timing allowed my body to return to its normal pace while using the extra energy to strike the ball almost effortlessly. Rhythm and balance were the foundations of Johnny's swing philosophy, and they were the words that I had discovered on my first day in Utopia.

I committed to my mental routine as I approached the first tee. I used Johnny's strategy of marking my balls with the letters SFT, giving me a visual reminder of my goal each time I looked down at the ball. I was prepared and at peace. Yet I stared down the fairway like a great warrior surveying his hunting grounds.

My front nine was solid. I shot two under, and it could easily have been lower. I had caught the leaders. I could smell blood.

As I approached the tenth tee, I was in the zone. I had birdied the tenth in each of the previous rounds. Then it happened. Someone in the gallery yelled, "I bet you can beat a fifteen on this hole."

I was caught off-guard. I had been completely engrossed in the round. It hadn't crossed my mind that it had been the tenth hole the last day in San Antonio that did me in. My first instinct was to yell back, but I tried to ignore the comment and the chuckles that rippled through the gallery.

I had been in control. But now I was both angry and scared.

I looked down the fairway and noticed for the first time the trees and trouble on the left. Instead of going with my game plan, I decided to change. I knew that if I could just get past this hole, I would be OK. I played protective. It was the first time all day that I stopped hunting and became the hunted.

I chose to hit a three-wood and play out to the right. It would mean a longer shot into the green, but I was just hoping for par at this point. I stood behind the ball and stared down the fairway.

A helicopter was heading our way. I could faintly hear an ambulance siren in the distance. Some kids were laughing and kidding around behind the gallery. It was the first time today I had noticed anything.

In spite of it all, I was determined to go through my routine. But I had no clear shot in mind, only one that would avoid trouble. I was sabotaging my talent. I felt pressure to get the shot over with, so I caved in and swung. I made a conservative swing. I pulled the shot hoping for a fade away from the trouble. But instead I got the "double cross." The ball landed deep in the trees. I couldn't believe it.

On the way to the ball I told myself to stay calm, to breathe deeply, and to embrace the pressure. I realized that I had played scared, and it made me mad. It was evident that the shot was caused by doubt, not a swing flaw. I was determined to take my medicine, accept the shot and move on. However, the adversity was just heating up. We found the ball, but it had come to rest between two roots of a large oak tree. I was about to come unglued when I looked up. I caught a glimpse of the sun's rays streaking through the limbs of this majestic oak. Wasn't it just a few days ago that I had sat under a tree similar to this and listened to a man call me to a new perspective? A calm came over my body. My perspective returned, and I realized I was OK. No matter what happened in this tournament, I was OK.

A rules official approached, and we discussed my options. It was clearly an unplayable lie, and a drop wasn't looking good. My other option was to return to the tee and take stroke and distance. If I returned to the tee and hit a good drive I would be laying three but would be farther up the fairway on this reachable par five. To everyone's surprise, I headed back to the tee.

The co-leaders, including the Lion, watched me trudge up the fairway towards them. I am sure everyone was feeling sorry for this poor old choke, but my fire was rekindled. I carried myself like a champion and showed no sign of giving in. As my competitors nodded in condolence, I smiled and said, "This is going to be a heck of a par."

I teed up the ball and stared down the fairway with a look of a gunfighter. I had a plan, and I attacked the plan with purpose. I went through my routine. I smoked the ball up the left side, hugging the fairway around the bend. I winked at my opponents and said, "I'll see you in the house, boys. Play well." The advantage they were looking for from this situation was hanging by a thread.

I had 240 to the green with bunkers left and water right. All I saw was the landing area, the shape and trajectory of the shot. I was back in the zone, having fun with this challenge. The ball flew true to its target and came to rest twenty-five feet from the pin. I could accept a bogey, but I had a par in my sights. I knew that a par here would rattle the guys behind me. I was loving this stage.

I saw the line, felt the distance, and trusted my stroke. As soon as the ball left my putter face, I knew it was in. The ball rattled into the cup for par as the crowd let out a raucous applause. No birdie received as much applause that day.

It was as though I had reached another gear. Everything was in hyper focus. Colors seemed to jump out, my strategy was clear, decisions were evident, and I was able to play the game of golf in front of the ball. My swing was but a distant memory. I birdied four more holes on the way to posting a sixty-six.

I knew when the round was over that I had accomplished my objective, with the exception of that one shot on the 10th. The other amazing thing was that once I told Travis and his playing partner that I would see them in the house, I never gave them another thought. I simply refused to give any power to the hype. My job had been simplified to that over which I had control. Simply focus on the checklist, see it, feel it, and trust it. What a way to play the game!

Travis played well, also. He stood on the 18th tee box needing a birdie to force a playoff. He loved this position. He seemed to thrive on the drama.

I signed my card and headed to the range, fully expecting that this tournament was going into sudden death. I knew Travis would birdie and in fact was hoping he would. I wanted to beat him at his best. Johnny taught me to never root against the other guy. He said that would cloud my heart. He was right; I compete best when I have a free heart.

On the way to the range, people both cheered me on and read me my last rites. Few gave me a chance against Travis. I was about to hit a few shots to stay warm when I heard a familiar voice call out my name. I thought about ignoring it since I was preparing for the chance of a lifetime. Then I heard it again and looked up to see Joe.

He was holding his young son, with his wife standing beside him holding the hand of their little girl. I walked over to the gallery ropes and was embraced by the whole family, three of whom I had never met. Before Joe could speak, his wife thanked me for giving them a new husband and father.

In the past two days Joe had buried the lies and made good on his old promise, "To love and to cherish, until death do us part." He had reconciled with his wife and kids and begun the process of proving to them that he was a new man. He told them that golf was out of his life until he mended his relationships at home and he had time to seek counsel on his new direction in life.

Joe told me that he had put a call into Johnny and that he and his family were heading to Utopia for a weeklong retreat. Johnny had told Joe that he had some business in Austin over the weekend, but he would be ready to go on Monday.

Johnny was here, I knew it. The note was from him. Maybe our time together had been good for him also. Maybe it had released him to return to a tournament site, a place that until now had only reminded him of the pain of the past.

That is why he taught that giving of self was so crucial in life. It returns like rain to the soul reviving the parched places.

An official tapped me on the shoulder and reported that Travis had indeed birdied. A playoff would begin on the 18th tee box in five minutes. A cart arrived to transport me to the tee box.

Joe looked into my eyes like no man had ever looked at me. It was a look stripped bare of all the masks that shroud most interaction between competing males. He said, "Thanks for letting God use you. I have my family back. I have my life back. These are the trophies I have so desperately needed. Now go and play like a champion, knowing you have won in the game of life. Remember, it is just a game."

A tournament trophy paled in comparison to the words I had just received. They were a trophy from God, a crystal that would forever sit in the throne room of grace.

His words lingered with me as I rode through the throngs of people to the tee box. It was all coming together, just as Johnny had explained. I was released. I was unencumbered. I was free to compete for the first time in my life. How simple. Golf is a game.

I was standing on the tee box as the sea parted. There coming towards me amid all the cheers was Travis the Lion. But I saw the look of a thousand masks as he stretched out his hand to shake mine. It wasn't just a game to him. It was life itself. He was not going to lose.

I knew in my heart that whatever the outcome of the playoff, he couldn't win, and I couldn't lose. The game was bigger than golf. I knew that I was free and that he was trapped. For me the reason they called him a Lion was not because he was a feared hunter; it was because he played with the ferociousness of a trapped and starving animal. No victory would release him from the trap, and no win would fill his appetite.

There was nothing that I had to fear, for I understood. I had been given wisdom.

He teed first and nailed it about 320 to the great thrill of his army of followers. It was my turn. I teed my ball. There glaring back at me was the mark, SFT. Three little letters. The power they gave was amazing. I struck my ball perfectly, hitting a hard fade, 280 to the right side of the fairway.

The hole was playing as a 590-yard par five. The green was surrounded on the front, left, and rear by water with a bail-out area to the right. The pin was tucked over on the right, away from the water but positioned to short-side those brave souls who went for it in two and missed on the right. This would leave them with an impossible pitch to a green that sloped severely away and towards the water.

My strategy was to lay up to my favorite yardage for my 56-degree wedge. I played my second shot to about ninety yards, hugging the left side of the fairway for the best angle to attack the pin. It was an unspectacular lay-up, which got very little applause from the gallery. In my mind it was perfect.

As Travis approached his ball, the noise began. The crowd almost in unison began to chant, "Go for it, go for it." He was about 270 to the flag, about 250 to clear the water. The distance was no big deal for him; it was the risk of the three sides of water that had his attention. Travis was not one to cave in to the crowd. He always played his game. But I could see the situation calling his name. He was playing a no-name. He hadn't missed a shot all day. The media was always pressing for more and more drama. The situation was ripe for a dramatic shot that would close the deal. He pulled out his three-metal and threw up some grass to check the wind. It was drifting to the right. This was a perfect shot for a long fade, but his natural shot was a draw.

The crowd stood motionless. You could see it on his face; he was ready to make history. The shot took off like a rocket. He lasered it right at the flag. The crowd exploded in cries of, "Go in! Go in!" The ball flew true until it reached its apex and began to drift slightly with the wind. It hit four feet right of the hole and its momentum carried it to the right fringe. To the gallery's horror and surprise, it trickled to the right, off the green and down the slope, severely short-siding Travis. He would be facing the toughest pitch on the course to a tight flag, with the green shooting downhill and away directly at the water.

I knew that he had gone against his plan. He had heard another voice that had won out. He was a great player, but he wasn't invincible.

I approached my shot with calm and confidence. However, the crowd was restless, running up to the green to see the misfortune of Travis. I chose a specific target and focused on the shape of the shot. I knew I had the perfect distance and that I would leave the ball left of the pin for an uphill putt. My see it, feel it, trust it checklist allowed me to hit despite the noise and movement. The shot was well struck, drifting slightly to the right with the wind. It landed six feet below the hole, spinning back to about eight feet. I received a small smattering of applause.

Travis knew he had a monumental task. He studied his options carefully. I saw only one option, pitching away from the flag. He saw another. He knew that pitching away from the flag would be a sign of cowardice. I knew he was trapped. He had to go for the win; it would be unforgivable if he didn't. I understood.

I could see what he was looking at. He walked up to the green and checked the flagstick to make sure it was set snug in the hole. He walked to the opposite side, then stood just behind the flagstick looking to his ball. He was taking dead aim at the pin. His only hope was to hit the stick. That is what he fully expected to do. If he hit the flag stick, he could make it or at least have the momentum of his ball checked. If he missed, he would have a forty-footer, minimum. If he didn't hit it perfectly, he could easily hit it in the lake.

Travis approached his shot. He chose a 60-degree wedge, opening it up slightly and playing his hands back to get the ball up quickly and make it land as softly as possible. I was impressed with his confidence. There was no margin for error, yet he saw nothing but the stick. His practice strokes were as smooth as silk; his rhythm and touch were otherworldly.

The Lion was ready. The gallery was breathless, anticipating the shot of the century. Travis swung and caught the ball ever so gently. It floated like a dandelion riding a summer breeze as it crested the hill and touched down with an enormous amount of spin for such a short shot. Because of the hill, it released following the initial skid and began to pick up momentum as it drew a bead for the stick. Travis jogged up the hill as the crowd's murmur grew to a roar. The ball was heading for the flag; perfection had been unleashed. The ball glanced off the stick, catching enough to arrest much of the momentum. But the hill's influence took effect and caused the ball to continue trickling until it came to rest about fifteen feet from the hole. He would have a fifteen foot left-to-right breaker for birdie. This was truly one of the gutsiest shots I had ever witnessed.

Instead of being stunned, I was impressed. I had just witnessed one of the great shots of all time. He had indeed called his shot. You could see it in his focused preparation. He was an artist. He knew what I had just learned. He knew how to let genius out. I simply watched and enjoyed from my front-row view. But I also knew what others didn't. He was trapped, and I was free.

How different I felt. I had never been able to think this way in the past. I had determined to root for him. I wanted him to play his best so I could beat him at his best. And I knew for the first time that I had genius inside as well. It was the springtime of my genius. I fully expected to hit great shots like that as well. Now I knew how. I had a way of letting it happen.

Travis studied his line like an engineer. He spoke with his caddy and came to a decision. He had a difficult putt, but it was makeable. He walked up to the hole and looked at the point he determined to be the entry point. He moved back to his ball and addressed the putt. Once again the crowd was still and quiet. His putter moved back. His body was like granite, motionless as his arms swung like a perfect pendulum. The ball traced a perfect arc for the hole. I watched as he raised his putter and arms as the ball was dead center with two feet to go. And then it dove right, catching the right lip, careening the ball a full 360 degrees, spitting it out on the entrance side. It was still teetering on the edge when it stopped. He dropped his arms in disbelief and looked at his caddy. The crowd began to yell, "Drop! Drop!" hoping the chant would coax the ball. But it stayed. Travis walked up to it and looked at it hopefully, but it was not to be. He tapped in and everyone began to move back up the fairway. They fully expected me to miss. They expected another playoff hole.

Travis attempted to slow them down, but the movement was uncanny. I placed my ball on the green. I knelt behind the ball to get the line. As I looked down the line something caught my eye in the gallery. There, right in my sightline, was Joe and his family. I saw his left arm around his wife, while holding his little girl in his right arm. Their son was standing in front of them, watching intently. Joe's wife was smiling.

It all came together in this scene. I had a putt to win a perishable trophy, but I was seeing an imperishable one. My eyes began to water to the point that I had to wipe them with my sleeve. But the tears began to stream down my face. I had been a part of eternity this week, and it had nothing to do with golf. This putt was meaningless in the big picture. I had been blessed by being used. I gave what Johnny gave. I passed love on in a competitive world.

I approached the putt but had to back off because of the tears that hung in my eyes, blurring my vision. I motioned for the caddy to bring me my towel. I wiped my face as though wiping away sweat. The crowd was quiet by now.

I approached my putt and saw the SFT on the ball. Suddenly I heard the knock. It was the knock of which Johnny had spoken. Destiny had come knocking on my door, and He wore a crown of thorns. I opened the door and I saw His face, felt His presence, and trusted His love. I simply said, "I have been expecting You; please come in. I have set an extra place at my dinner table."

The words that were upon His lips were the same as those that Johnny had read from the Good Book last Sunday, "Put out into the deep water and let down the nets for a catch."

I knew it was time; time to go where no one else had gone. It was time to move out into the deep, a place beyond tradition, a place of buried lies and unearthed truth. It was time to move to a place beyond my comfort zone, but a place of security because the voice came from within the boat.

I walked to the edge of the green where my caddy stood holding my bag. I handed him my traditional putter for the last time. I reached into the bag and pulled out the Face-On putter.

As I walked back to my ball you could hear a murmur among

the few spectators who had remained at the green. Those who were walking back up the fairway stopped and began to migrate back to the green out of curiosity. Travis had a look of confusion on his face that changed to shock as I approached my putt face-on.

In the past week I had experienced a rebirth. A revolution had begun within my soul. I knew this putt was to be the start of a revolution as well. And while it would look like a putting revolution to the world, it would forever be for me a symbol of the eternal truth that had set me free. I would never contend as before. For now I had a purpose and calling that went beyond success.

No longer would I live with the fear of failure or as a prisoner of tradition. My scoreboard had changed. While most dreams culminate with winning, my dream pressed deeper. It would take me to a place beyond success, a place where victory would be but a watering hole on the way to an eternal destination.

I took a practice stroke standing face-on to the target. I was relieved to feel the freedom of the face-on stroke that I had experienced in Utopia with the cowboys. I placed the putter face behind the ball while tracing a line to the hole with my eyes. I looked at the hole as I began my stroke.

I saw, felt, trusted, and stroked the putt of my life.

Utopia is defined as a place of mythical perfection. As the ball rolled toward the hole, I knew differently. Utopia was indeed real. It was a place in my heart. By the grace of God, it was a place that I would endeavor to live. It was a place where the voice of truth resides. It was a place of eternal trophies.

EPILOGUE

S o there lingers a question …
On the surface you want to know, "Did he make the putt?"
But the heart responds with, "Does it really matter?"

Your heart wants more — much more. It's pressing to go deeper. It longs for a personal sacred journey. Like the young golfer your heart wants to "push out into the deep." It desires Joe's reconciliation. It longs for Johnny's wisdom and a life with margin. It seeks significance. Above all your heart craves for hope — hope for more. There has to be more.

I understand. And that's why this story was written. It was written for your heart. And now you too, stand at the fork in the road. To the right is a conventional, safe village … to the left is Utopia, a place of buried lies and rescued dreams.

Utopia is a real village in the Hill Country of Texas, about eighty miles west of San Antonio. The golf course exists; the oak tree is there; the river beckons you to "wet a line;" delicious fried food abounds at the café; the cemetery awaits your buried lies. And if you look closely you will find a Johnny or two.

I hope you will make a trek to our "field of dreams" someday. But in the meantime, here is a first step to the "more" your heart longs for. This book is but a beginning. Join me at www.linksofutopia .com to continue your journey. The answer to your heart's yearning could begin there. Here is what you will find:

- The answer to "Did he make the putt?" You just may be surprised ...
- A place to bury your lies and begin your sacred journey ...
- A companion study guide for personal or small group study, allowing you to dig more deeply into the principles found in the book ...
- A plan for becoming like Johnny in your world. We have special discounts on multi-packs of this book waiting for you if you choose to use it to encourage others.
- A current listing of our retreats, events, and other resources for your journey ...
- More about Face-On putting
- A free on line video library of golf and sacred journey coaching from several of our country's top instructors who embody Johnny ...

www.linksofutopia.com
210 – 867 – 3634
"Continue the Journey"

A personal invitation from Tom Lehman (British Open Champion, 2006 Ryder Cup Captain), Scott Simpson (U.S. Open Champion), Larry Mize (Master's Champion), Stan Utley (PGA Tour winner, Top 10 Instructor, Golf Digest), Steve Lowery (PGA Tour winner), and Dick Coop (PGA Tour Mental Game Coach):

Epilogue

When we read this book something profound happened. This story was personal. We found ourselves in the story over and over. It stirred deep places, awakened dormant emotions, and revealed lies that have held us back. The words challenged us in very thought provoking ways to be revolutionary in how we live our lives from now to eternity. In Chapter 8 Dr. Cook posed the question, "Where have all the Johnnies gone ... who teaches wisdom these days?" For us this was a calling out, a direct challenge to embody the character of Johnny by seeking ways to encourage another human being with wisdom.

A simple first step for us was to get this book in the hands of those in our sphere of influence and then to have margin in our lives in case the book opens the door to a deep conversation.

Would you join us on this mission to spread the message of this book? If so, please join us in this "Johnny Project" by logging on to www.linksofutopia.com to order a 10 pack to distribute to your friends, family business, or golf outing.

Thanks for joining us on the journey!

ABOUT THE AUTHOR

Author, speaker, and peak performance consultant, Dr. David Cook is on a mission to coach the eternal legacies of men.

Moving men from success to significance is his passion.

Golf's Sacred Journey is a novel based on Dr. David Cook's more than twenty-five years of experience. He has served as mental training coach for the San Antonio Spurs during their first two NBA World Championships, worked with over one hundred PGA Tour players, and has counseled individuals and teams from the NFL, MLB, Olympics, and colleges across the United States. David began his career at the University of Kansas, after receiving his PhD in applied sport psychology from the University of Virginia under sports psychology pioneer, Bob Rotella. Featured at two National PGA Teaching and Coaching Summits, he has also been named "Top 10 Mental Game consultant" by *Golf Digest Magazine*.

David bridges the gap between sports and business and is considered one of the country's top peak performance consultants and seminar leaders. Teaching principles that help business leaders achieve their fullest potential in the face of adversity, Dr. Cook enables people from every walk of life to deliver superior performance. His business clients include Fortune 100 companies, such as Exxon/Mobil, Sprint, HP/Compaq, Texas Instruments, and American Express.

Throughout his career, David has remained focused on coaching the eternal legacies of men and is now helping others to join *Golf's Sacred Journey* through three day *Sacred Journey Retreats* in Utopia, Texas. These unique events deliver lessons that can be applied to sports, business, and life.

Married over twenty-eight years, David and his wife, Karen, have two daughters and live in the Hill Country of Texas.

To learn more about David's retreats, speaking events, audiotapes, DVDs, and other resources for the journey, including multipacks of this book for friends, families, or local golf outings, visit *www.linksofutopia.com* or call 210.867.3634.

Golf's Sacred Journey, the Sequel

7 More Days in Utopia

David L. Cook, author of the bestselling Golf's Sacred Journey

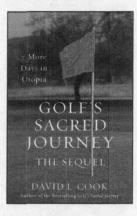

Golf is more than a game. Behind every stroke and ace, there are hours of practice. Before every trophy, there is sacrifice. At every driving range, there are successes and failures. And inside every golfer, there is a story.

In *Golf's Sacred Journey, the Sequel*, the book that follows bestselling *Golf's Sacred Journey*, professional golfer Luke Chisholm returns to his winsome and wise mentor, Johnny Crawford, for what he's best at: advice. This time, Luke needs help of a different sort. He needs guidance on playing in the most difficult golf tournament in the world: the U.S. Open. Victory is in sight.

From bestselling author and performance psychologist Dr. David Cook, *Golf's Sacred Journey, the Sequel* is the fascinating byproduct of counseling thousands of athletes over the decades—from PGA champions to Olympic athletes. His expertise weaves throughout this suspenseful and memorable sequel.

Luke's story unfolds from the practice course of Utopia, Texas, to the fairways of the U.S. Open. It's there that T.K., Luke's rival, re-enters the picture. Their rivalry comes to a head at the U.S. Open. Their clash is epic, the payoffs and costs are great.

In this memorable book, readers will acquire lessons about golf and life that they never expected as Luke and T.K. overcome gripping fears, trials, and brokenness as they pursue their God-given dreams. *Golf's Sacred Journey, the Sequel* will deeply inspire readers both on and off the green.

This is a story of two golfers. This is a story of redemption. And in the end, it's not just about a game.

Available in stores and online!